CORTINA JENELLE CALDWELL

how to HEAL THE PLANET from wherever you are

Leaning into the Cosmic + Planetary Link Between Ancestral Healing, Collective Liberation + Creative Entrepreneurship

How to Heal the Planet from Wherever You Are: Leaning Into the Cosmic + Planetary Link Between Ancestral Healing, Collective Liberation + Creative Entrepreneurship

This book was typeset in Montserrat along with Hussar Ekologiczy and Playlist Script used as display typefaces. Cover illustration by Cortina Jenelle Caldwell. Exterior and interior illustration elements sourced from Canva, Inc. of Sydney, Australia.

Publishing and Design:

To send correspondence to the authors of this book, send letters to
Attention: Cortina Jenelle Caldwell c/o Good News Ink
125 S. Lexington Avenue, Unit 101A, Asheville, NC 28801

Ordering Information: Quantity sales. Special discounts are available on quantity purchases by corporations, associations, and others. For details, contact the publisher at the address above, Orders by U.S. trade bookstores and wholesalers..

Third Edition, July 2025.

For more info about Good News Ink or to book Cortina Jenelle Caldwell for an event or interview, visit: itsgoodnews.space or email goodnewsinkpublishing@gmail.com

how to

HEAL

THE PLANET

from wherever you are

FREE MINI-JOURNAL
FOR REFLECTION + NOTETAKING

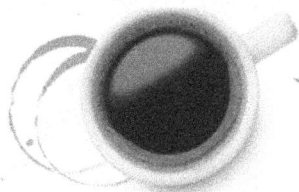

mini REFLECTION JOURNAL

CORTINA JENELLE CALDWELL

how to HEAL THE PLANET from wherever you are

PROCEEDS FROM THIS BOOK PLANT(ED) GOOD SEEDS

OSHANNA teaches principles of permaculture, biomimicry and holistic wellness through land access projects, popular education circles and creative facilitation. OSHANNA is a faith-rooted community where nature is the classroom, nature is the co-facilitator and often, nature is the source of our study materials. Our methodology is to use emergent and inquiry-based approach to education, reinforcing practices of inclusion, cooperation, design, preservation and community using a project- or residency-based delivery for students of all ages.

For our in-person programs, you'll find us on farms, in urban outdoor spaces, by rivers, trekking through forests and near scenic byways. Our students establish a reciprocal relationship with the land and to create an understanding of themselves as part of the natural world. All programs and curricula are designed by Cortina Jenelle Caldwell, author of *How to Heal the Planet from Wherever You Are: Leaning into the Cosmic + Planetary Link Between Ancestral Healing, Collective Liberation + Creative Entrepreneurship.*

NATURE IS OUR LEGACY.
#sojournoflight

OSHANNA

TABLE OF CONTENTS

TABLE OF CONTENTS

This book is dedicated to God --
without their many divine interventions,
I would not be here today. I also
dedicate this book to the planet,
my first true home, my Divine Mother
and the greatest teacher I have ever
known. Your rivers and lakes baptized
my right to exist, your forests and jungles
whispered their wisdom, your mountains
and soil the bones, flesh + blood of my
ancestors...and the wind, the magical
matriarch of movement, reminding me
that just because you cannot see a thing,
does not mean it isn't real.

[For a full list of sources cited and referenced in this
book, please visit: itsgoodnews.space/source-list]

SERVE THE PLANET

Our deepest fear is not that we are inadequate. Our deepest fear is that we are powerful beyond measure. It is our light not our darkness that most frightens us. We ask ourselves, who am I to be brilliant, gorgeous, talented and fabulous? Actually, who are you not to be? You are a child of God. Your playing small does not serve the world. There's nothing enlightened about shrinking so that other people won't feel insecure around you. We were born to make manifest the glory ofGod that is within us.It's not just in some of us; it's in everyone. And as we let our own light shine, we unconsciously give other people permission to do the same. As we are liberated from our own fear, our presence automatically liberates others.

Marianne Williamson

[A Return to Love]

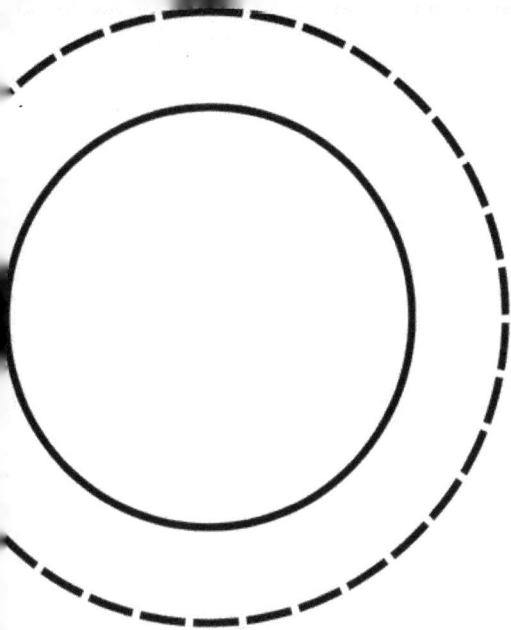

INVOCATION

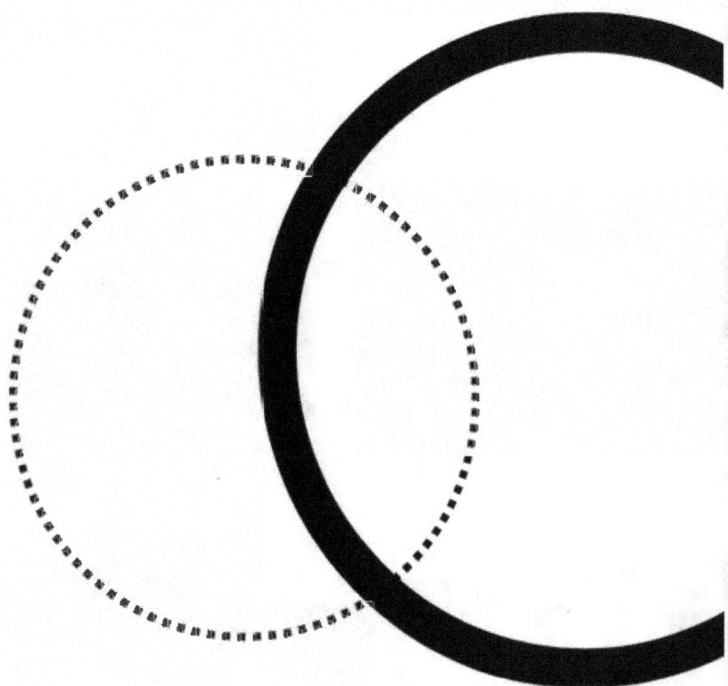

CALL IT IN

Calling all forces for good, calling in the elemental energies, the spirits of the land and of the creatures that walk it, the spirits of the waters, and those that dwell within, the spirits of the air, and those who float and take wing on the wind. Calling to the ancient guardians of this planet, and of its peoples. Calling on the long-sleeping force of the "mythological" beings of old. Calling on the directions: North, South, East, West. Call on the Above and the Below. Calling on Center. See us through this time in a powerful and protective way. Give us courage and inner calm, foresight and preparedness for the battles we are righting, and wins for the ones that are ahead. Give us clarity to see the moments of peace, and to draw strength for our love and fortitude. Offer us answers in our dreams, and support in our waking. Calling on the Great Mystery, the benevolent powers of creation. Help us tap our higher calling, our magic and our bravery for the days to come, and for today.

Earthdancer

[2018]

Congratulations on your forward moving action to make two of the best investments you'll ever make in your life - one in yourself and one for the planet - both of which are gifts that will keep giving back. As I start to prepare you for the journey we're about to take together, I want to name some things that are important to acknowledge early on as we set the stage for the work that will happen between these pages and out in the world, through your inspired action. I stand with you, beloved. Are you ready to begin?

First, throughout this book you will see me refer to the planet as Mother Earth, Gaia, Pachamama or the Wheel of Fortune. I use these terms interchangeably as a nod to the different embodiments that the planet takes with a slightly different energetic imprint to call in the same "body". In my studies of history, culture and spirituality over the last two decades, I have also heard Earth referred to as a masculine energy by some and it is not something that resonates with me or my lineage as far as I know it at this time. I will also say that with this majestic planet we get to call home being one of evolution and change that perhaps at one time it was more of a masculine energy, but as I connect in with my own Earth practices, what is reflected back to me is a Divine Mother who simply wants the best for her children. She picks no favorites (i.e. plants, animals, fungi, humans, elements, etc) and knows that each child brings its own unique magic to the family and will need its own unique kind of love, protection and parenting. I believe it is her hope for us that we correct some of the mistakes we have made in going against her before we have to endure more tough love to finally get the lesson. I pray we get it soon.

Secondly, I am no one's guru but my own. As are you. I come with my fair share of heartbreaks, achievements, tragedies and wildly amazing experiences all in one mixed bag. The only thing setting apart author from reader in this case is my cadence. It is not my goal to entice more followers, but to build up authentic leaders. My curiosity started off young. As a child of teenage parents, I always felt like I had something to prove and went about researching, reading, traveling, observing and testing my theories about why I was here and what life was all about. As someone who values wisdom, I hope that my life can be of service as a way of paying-it-forward. So while I'm not your guru, I am a results expert. I know what I know because of the blood, sweat, tears and TIME to refine the strategies, wisdom and tools passed to me. What you find in these pages is also up to your own discourse and discovery. You will find a link for references and research a few pages back. And even if you're just curious for now, I hope you too will become an expert in your lived experience and offer your wisdom, in your own creative, unique way, to the world or to your people. I believe that's how we heal the planet from wherever you are.

Finally, I fully respect that time is a limited resource (which I touch on in the "Time is True Wealth" chapter) so I have designed this book to get straight to the point. Some chapters also offer pages for reflection or doodling - choose your own adventure - so that you can start forming your playbook ASAP. There are also toolkits to support your meetings, a bridge to social media to keep the conversation going and a free mini-journal if you need more space. Read at the pace that is right for you and trust the process. Finishing the book is not the end...it's only the beginning.

Cortina Jenelle Caldwell

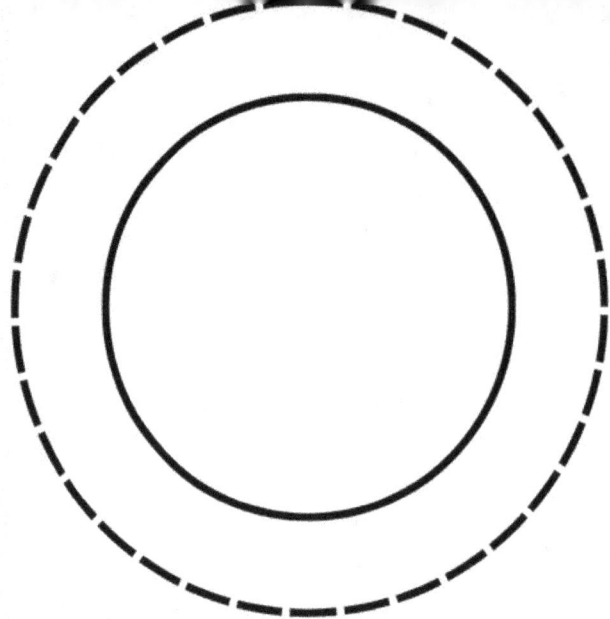

START WHERE YOU ARE

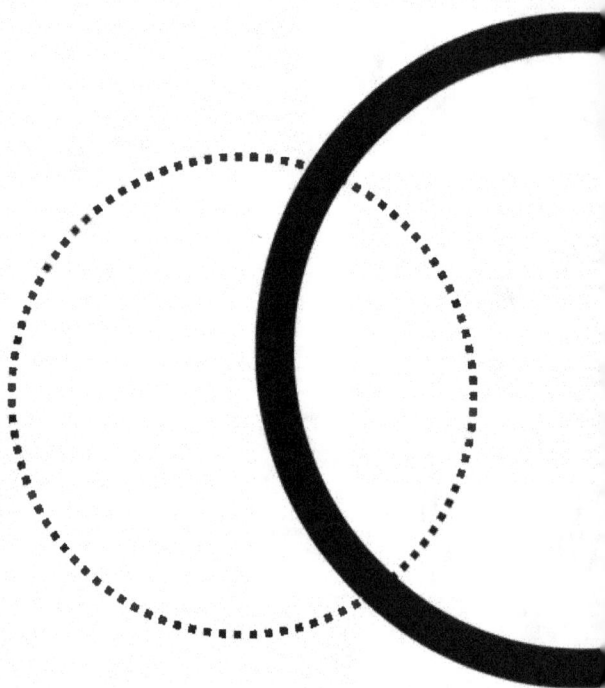

HEALING THE PLANET
BEGINS WITH YOU

What comes to mind when you think about the word healing? Do you imagine a doctor, a nurse? Do you envision an herbalist or kitchen witch? Do you imagine services you would like to book and have done? Or do you turn your attention to your very own body? Let me relieve you, none of those answers are wrong, however, over the years in my work as a holistic coach, healer and Kemetic yoga instructor, there is an answer I hear from my clients much less than any others and that answer is the body. Why? Many of us are in a perpetual loop of seeking answers outside of ourselves and even for those of us that are actively trying to unlearn the programs that have us turn away from ourselves and look to others for our worth, our value, to complete us or to fix us, it can be a tedious, messy process to find our way back to Self.

One of my favorite proverbs or life motto is "as above so below, as within so without" Meaning that our actions are a reflection of what we value (or not), our reality is a reflection of our innermost beliefs and our communities then as well as the (state of the) planet is a reflection of how we engage with our own homes, Mother archetypes

6

and the way we show up in relationships in general. For example - have you ever wondered what the home of a person who litters looks like? Have you ever had a conversation or studied the values of those who make GMO foods or dump waste in the oceans? Those are just two examples, but you get the point - how we treat the planet is TRULY a reflection of how we treat ourselves, and in my opinion the climate crisis is never going to shift if people do not have an internal revelation and start caring more about how they treat their own bodies, minds, hearts and homes. Whether we like it or not, the two are absolutely interconnected and I'm here to bring that perspective to the table. I'm all about environmental justice (see my chapter on "Earth service"), but once again I say - it is not just an external, "outside of us issue". We have to, collectively, have a complete reorientation to waste reduction, consumption, capitalism, etc which may mean releasing or replacing some creature comforts. We have to be willing to hold ourselves accountable to our ecosystems, which means first realizing that we are ALL apart of one. We have to take the conversation beyond recycling and composting to actual reverse engineer simple solutions or actions that we can take every day to reduce our dependence on plastics, gather groups for litter cleanup, upcycling clothing, engage in and choose to by from Certified B Corps or fair trade, living wage businesses. There is alot that can be done. Yet none of it will matter or last if you do not remember your place in this fragile web of life and step outside of your human meat suit for a moment to remember that being on Earth means you do not have the luxury of only thinking about yourself. Your children and

the entire galaxy

depends on it.

No pressure.

HOW TO USE ASTROLOGY
AS A COMPASS

Speaking of galaxy, one of my absolute favorite things to do is to lay on the ground outside on a starry night and stare up at the stars and planets. A few years ago someone introduced me to the *Star Walk 2* (only on iOS, I believe) app and my mind was BLOWN. Not only could I continue my habit of stargazing, but now I could bring my inner researcher into the circle and geek out on the names asteroids, find planets and zodiac constellations in the sky. Then in a moment of wanting to blow my students minds one evening under a Full Moon Lunar Eclipse, I pulled out the app to explore not only the sky above, but the sky beneath us. Talk about spooked! It was such a simple action, but in that moment I had reminded them that we are on living, breathing planet (or as I said it a rolling ball hurtling through outer space), perpetually dancing with a ball of light (Sun) and a manifestation of the void (Moon) in mathematically perfect angles at all times, giving us the four seasons and infinite forms of life. Talk about a reality check, no? When you take a moment to zoom out and remember all that you are apart, the petty drama and little inconveniences do not seem to matter as much as the gift of being HERE, now.

HOW TO USE ASTROLOGY AS A COMPASS

So, if you haven't already, I would highly recommend that a good starting point for this journey of ours (or really at any time that it resonates for you) is to learn and become familiar with your natal (birth) chart. I can confidently tell you that astrology - knowing who I am and what I was here to do, my past life gifts, my wounded areas, my gifts, my relationship patterns - saved my life. Suddenly, I wasn't looking for belonging in the world around me anymore because I truly had a home amongst the REAL stars. I know who I am and I am clear about what I am here to do and what my unique path is going to look like. Even though I first started studying the planets in school just as a personal interest, I started taking workshops and trained up in research + ancestral guidance about 10 years ago. There are many sites out there that will provide you with a free birth chart so do some research and make that an actionable item from this chapter. If you need support making sense of it, you can download my podcast episodes on "Unpacking Astrology" to get a sense of what things all mean or schedule a reading with myself or my circle of trust which includes Virginia Rosenberg and Liz Gunn Astrology. On a final note here, I will also name that I know there've been many attempts to discredit astrology and name astronomy as the "true science", but let me big up my ancestors for a moment and remind us all that astronomy, created just 300 years ago, would not be possible if not for the work of the Ancient Kemetic scholars and scientists, the Dogon specifically, who first charted the sky in 3000 BC. For them, astrology wasn't a career path for some, it was a way of life, guiding the rhythms of seed sowing, harvest, celebration, union and so much more. I give thanks.

THE CHALLENGE
OF PATRIARCHY

As mentioned in earlier chapters and as I will continue to reinforce throughout this book, my writing is informed both by my lived experience as well as my scholarly studies, research and critical analysis of information given to me. Yet, here and only here will I share a list with you of some ways that I identify in an attempt to make it clear from which margins, intersections and perspectives I am speaking. I identify as a Black, indigenous nonbinary, Queer, androgynous, Two-Spirit female-bodied, free-Spirited, holistic, entrepreneur, creative professional, yoga instructor, tree hugging vegan-ish, humanitarian and a member of Captain Planet's mod squad. In other words, no boxes for me, please and thank you. Being that for much of my upbringing and into adult, I was seeking out belonging, love and purpose under every nook and cranny, there were MANY things that I tried, tried on as well as many spiritual practices, religions and transformational experiences I got invited into. In all of these spaces, I had to leave some aspect of myself or my identity out of the room, not feeling "safe" (a word I used to use) to bring in all of me because how can you fit in if you create disruption everywhere you go, by nature?

One of the most important things I noticed was the pattern of treatment of those that were female. To be even more specific, even if there were other aspects of my identity that the men in the room shared, energetically, socially and economically I was automatically at a disadvantage. I was not and am not disadvantaged because I do not adopt victimizing language as "I am's", however, because of how things were set up systemically as well as how people internalized a white supremacist culture (check the resource list for more on unpacking this if this is a new term for you), I supposedly did not have any power. I say all of this to say that the same system telling female-bodied people that they have less power are the same who benefit from the billion-trillion dollar beauty, wellness, fitness and diet industries. To say that just because I was born in this body meant I had no or less power, or that I was innately sinful seemed like a mindgame to me so I set out to investigate and deprogram that shit. For me, the dots didn't start connecting until I was doing my Black liberation, economic development, spiritual tradition work all layered at once...which is when something clicked for me. Many of the cultures, in my lineage and many around the Diaspora and native lands are a matrilineal people meaning the family name, customs, wealth, etc are passed down through the mother. How had this information been forgotten I wondered? To put it simply, colonization and imperialism has been firing on all cylinders for thousands of years to find all the ways to disturb the peace, divide + conquer and to keep us off balance. That included the invention of race, making people (especially women + children) property and creating hierarchy to diminish our sovereignty + divinity.

AUTHENTICITY:
PURPOSE TO PATHWAY

So, you feeling a way yet? I know when I started to piece the whole puzzle together for myself, I was deeply enraged and it took me months to unpack and unravel all of my feelings around all these problems - racial justice, gender justice, reproductive justice, environmental justice, animal rights, food sovereignty, indigenous protection, poverty, housing crisis, educational reform - that I once thought had their own unique needs. In my processing with friends, my therapist, mentors, ancestors and spirit guides (y'all, I did ALOT of processing around this), I finally came to an understanding of course that the appearance of these issues being separate seemed like a great way to keep us busy and apart yet never seeing and they were all connected to the same root problem - we had given our power away. Now, before your chest gets tight, journey with me for a moment here because it is not my way to make assumptions or to tell you what you think, only you can do that. What I am saying is that collectively, the systems that were put into place to "help us" or "aid us", seem to be benefitting more when we are unwell, unhappy, imbalanced, disempowered and too tired.

I could rattle off a list of five small actions that would have a big impact for each of the community challenges that I name above, but I won't. Why? Because I am not a guru and it's not up to me to fix this on my own which is why I'm sitting in circle (in a way) with every single person who is holding a copy of this book. I am here to activate you and to remind you that you are in the best and most perfect position to make a difference in this world and on this planet simply by getting to the business of developing your inner world so that you are equipped and ready when you're called to action. So, it is your authenticity that I'm most interested in. Back in 2016, I gave a talk on authenticity at the Lead Differently Conference put on by the Society of Human Resource Management in Asheville, NC and in 2013, I did my Masters' thesis/research project on "Branding Authenticity" so I'm not just saying it because the word is trendy now. I have been courting authenticity for a long time and I know with everything in my bones that if you're willing to show up as your truest, most benevolent version, flaws and all, and welcome others who are doing the same but working a different lane than you, I can guarantee you the solutions we could all come up with together would literally be out of this world. And that's EXACTLY what the planet needs. We are in the Age of Aquarius, which is essentially the sign of collective, community, cooperation and revolution, which means there is no greater time than right now to see how folks in other industries, professions or countries have been solving their problems. I'll add that for me, Creative Facilitation has been a total game changer for my clients so check out "Decolonize Your Meetings" or "Open Space Technology under the Toolkit section for more on that.

TAKING PERSONAL INVENTORY

So! Here we are. You have officially arrived at the final chapter in this section and I know you are probably relieved to jump ahead to some other parts. Not because I gave some extra doses of truth serum in there, I'm sure. But because I know how daunting and overwhelming doing our personal work can seem if we have no experience, no relationship with ourselves or no support. I get it and I know it all too well. You may have remembered me mentioning some folks in my circle of trusted colleagues as well as those that helped me process my rage (and grief, sadness, hope) about the state of the world, yes? Let that be a seed planted for you for the support you need to arrive at the exact right time. Now, before you go out trying to get everyone on board with the inner work you're doing and telling them I sent you knocking because we have to hurry up and save the planet....breathe. From a calm and grounded place, take out a piece of paper, putting yourself in the middle with a circle around you and then start making a brain map using the questions on the next page as a guide to get you started. If someone or something is actively in your life, make it closer to you and if infrequent, further away.

14

Here are the questions to help guide you, beloved:
- What does support mean or look like to me?
- Where is it difficult for me to ask for support?
- Who are the people closest to me? What sort of support do they provide or offer to my wellbeing?
- What natural resources support me (i.e. parks, hikes, drinking water, house, farm, produce, etc)?
- What does money support/make possible in my life?
- What practices support me when I'm stressed?
- How does my education (of any kind) support me?
- What professionals or service providers support me (i.e. therapist, coach, mentor, pastor, tax advisor, etc)?
- How do I support and nurture my spiritual life?
- What groups am I apart of that provide support (or could I be apart of in the future)?

There is no wrong way to do this, which is a key reason you don't see an example map here. You can draw a map, you can make a list, whatever works for you. Just DO make a commitment to take this step as a practice in getting to know yourself even deeper and understanding where you are supported or illuminating where you aren't. You can keep adding, or taking away, or do this seasonally. Make it something that is alive for you so that when you are ready to make your rules of engagement, you find support with ease and not struggle. Please also remember that this work we've started doing in this section is a practice in doing the inner work so you can show up how you're being called in the external work and this is a step not to be skipped. When we skip our internal work, we can cause harm to ourselves or others and at the end of the day, it's not a sprint, it's a marathon.

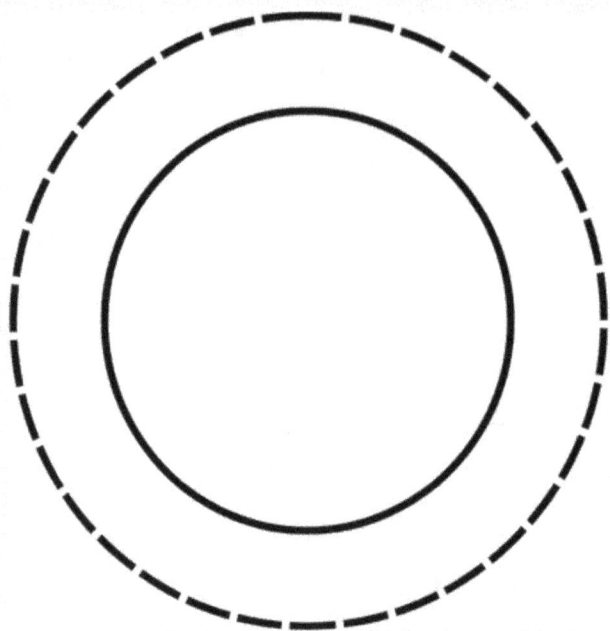

INDIGENOUS ROOTS

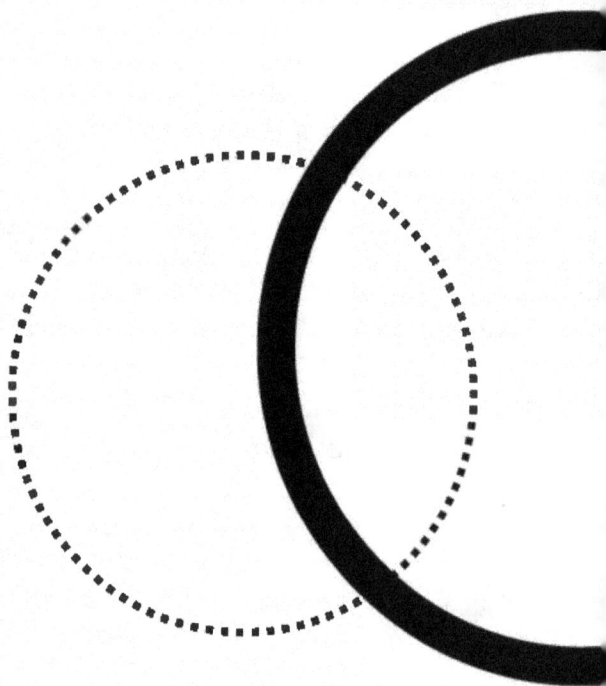

WISE COUNCIL

Although the understanding of the village and tending to the hearth as the center of a community or home has been part of many cultures for thousands of years, including my own lineages, it was devouring *Chicken Soup for the Teenage Soul* by Jack Canfield and Mark Victor Hansen in high school that awoken the power of a collective voice in circle within me. At the time, I hadn't experienced anything as powerful as that. The sharing of stories, the reflections, wisdom and insights from those stories and finding myself on pages with people whose path had never crossed mine affirmed for me that we were deeply connected, even while living out our individuality. In my early adulthood, I was having a moment of reflecting on my life (as I tend to do during the Winter season especially) as well as trying to find the missing links in my ancestry. I had a deep and sudden urge to connect with them because I felt that if I knew more about them, maybe all of my quirks would make more sense. In my search for them, I found myself, and little did I know it then, but my life started to become more organized in "circles" as opposed to the separatist, hierarchal lines I had been programmed to operate in.

As I started to look around at my life and journey, I realized that I had actually been born into a circle, or village. In many ways, it was imbalanced, dysfunctional and a cauldron for chaos, yet as with life, it was a mixed bag. Because of the fact that I had teenage parents, there were aunties, cousins, neighbors, teachers, friends and godparents involved with my upbringing. Although I do not hold the same belief systems or lifestyles that many of my relatives do, I recognize that the village that raised me planted a seed that would later blossom as I was having my first "baby", or business. I birthed Artists Designing Evolution (adé PROJECT) in 2018 and from inception, I knew it needed to be a cooperative so that the principles of equity and belonging were balanced. Based on what know culturally and historically, I knew that I wanted to be at round tables, not exclusive ones. As my work with adé PROJECT evolved, I was able to make change in my own hometown and take that work on the road, internationally. When researching cooperatives, I came across *Collective Courage: A History of African-American Cooperative Economic Thought and Practice* by Dr. Jessica Gordon Nembhard, as well as introducing her at a summit I presented at and I knew it was a signal to the universe that I was on the right track. As we move toward systems and a society that has decentralized its power and equalized decision-making to those most impacted by inequity, I believe down in my bones that we are returning to village building and circle work once again. As you move from your inner work to external action, review your support brain map from the previous section. Get clear on those that do or will support the authentic you and decide what you will build together.

THE NGUZO SABA

Kwanzaa is one of my absolute favorite holidays and one that I initially rejected in childhood because it came with ridicule and more being different. While everybody else around me was talking Santa Claus and Christmas, our household was talking about Kwanzaa and the Kwanzaa-man. Ridiculous, I KNOW. I'm laughing out loud as I write about this. In me sharing this though, there are so many gems for you to pull out but two important ones:

- Things in your life are not happening TO you, they are happening FOR you; and
- The things you experience in life are preparing you for your future. All things are a seed until cultivated.

I first came to know of Kwanzaa by someone who was a Five Percenter (see source list for more on this), which in short held the belief that being Black was both original and supreme. So I spent a lot of time hearing about what Black people should and shouldn't be doing, reading the Holy Qur'an and being anti-holidays...but the seed had been planted. I reconnected with Kwanzaa as I was building adé PROJECT and knew I wanted these principles to be the values of our coop organization.

More importantly, I wanted to constantly check my life + make these values by which I lived my life daily, not just when the Kwanzaa holiday rolled around December 26-January 1 each year. Each year consistently since then, it has been a beautiful time of celebration, reflection and giving back to the community for my organizations, businesses and just who I am as a person. For the most part, I have completely separated from Christmas because it's not something I culturally align with. Now that I have made that decision for myself as an adult I have peace in being able to carry the torch for my ancestors and I get excited thinking of new gatherings to curate each year. If that's something that interests you, be sure you're on my mailing list to see what I'm up to!

The concept of Kwanzaa was originally created in 1966, founded in collaboration, and coined by Dr. Maulana Karenga as a response to decades of work on Africana studies. Dr. Karenga researched African harvest celebrations and combined aspects of several different celebrations, such as those of the Ashanti and those of the Zulu, to form the foundation of Kwanzaa. The name Kwanzaa is derived from the phrase "matunda ya kwanza" which means first fruits, or harvest, in Swahili. Celebrations often include singing and dancing, storytelling, poetry reading, African drumming, and feasting. Dr. Karenga is a professor and chairman of Africana Studies at California State University. He moved from inspired action to coin the holiday in response to the Watts Riots in Los Angeles in 1965 as a way to bring African-Americans together as a community. The seven core principles of Kwanzaa are known as the Nguzo Saba. Kwanzaa is celebrated globally by millions each year.

Umoja: Unity | To strive for and maintain unity in the family, community, nation, and race. **This is the first principle of Kwanzaa, celebrated during holiday on December 26th each year.**

In the space below, reflect on what this principle means to you, or use this space for end-of-year/new year vision boarding about unity.

Kujichagulia: Self-Determination | To define ourselves, name ourselves, create for ourselves, and speak for ourselves. **This is the second principle of Kwanzaa, celebrated during holiday on December 27th each year.**

In the space below, reflect on what this principle means to you, or use this space for end-of-year/ new year vision boarding about **self-determination**.

Ujima: Collective Work and Responsibility | To build and maintain our community together and make our brothers' and sisters' problems our problems and solve them together. **This is the third principle of Kwanzaa, celebrated during holiday on December 28th each year.**

In the space below, reflect on what this principle means to you, or use this space for end-of-year/ new year vision boarding about collective work.

Imani: Faith | To believe with all our heart in our people, our parents, our teachers, our leaders, and the righteousness and victory of our struggle. This is the fourth principle of Kwanzaa, celebrated during holiday on December 29th each year.

In the space below, reflect on what this principle means to you, or use this space for end-of-year/ new year vision boarding about faith.

Ujamaa: Cooperative Economics | To build and maintain our own stores, shops, and other businesses and to profit from them together. **This is the fifth principle of Kwanzaa, celebrated during holiday on December 30th each year.**

In the space below, reflect on what this principle, or use this space for end-of-year/ new year vision boarding about cooperative economics.

Nia: Purpose | To make our collective vocation the building and developing of our community in order to restore our people to their traditional greatness. **This is the sixth principle of Kwanzaa, celebrated during holiday on December 31st each year.**

In the space below, reflect on what this principle means to you, or use this space for end-of-year/ new year vision boarding about purpose.

Kuumba: Creativity | To do always as much as we can, in the way we can, in order to leave our community more beautiful and beneficial than we inherited it. This is the seventh principle of Kwanzaa, celebrated during holiday on January 1st each year.

In the space below, reflect on what this principle means to you, or use this space for end-of-year/ new year vision boarding about creativity.

YOU ARE A DIVINE COSMIC FORCE

There have been many attempts to distance astronomy from astrology claiming that astronomy is the "true science" but it is worth noting that at one point the two were one conjoined practice. The focuses of astronomy - solar flares, asteroids, planetary and galactic explorations - were not so separate from the spirituality of astrology - energies of planets, Moon cycles, examining zodiac constellations for personal understanding, etc. As I started to get deeper into my studies of the galaxy, planets and zodiac, I began to ask myself - could this be another example of divide and conquer? Were astronomy and astrology divine counterparts...a masculine and feminine perspective to the understanding of Creation and life itself? Yet as studying the sky (above or beneath) will do, the questions just made room for more questions.
What did end up becoming inherently clear was that the "gods and goddesses" of Ancient Kemet, while clearly differentiated from each other in some respects and not as clearly in others, also each represent an aspect of this abstract concept "Neteru," as Names (or expressions) of Creator/Creation. In other words, each of the planets and zodiac constellation were assigned a Neteru, which in

which in their representation would also give a blueprint to understanding who we are, taking our place in the stars and therefore understanding our significance to the planet. While astrology is not an area of expertise for me, I make space for it in this book in hopes to exhibit that reclaiming our creative authority is dependent upon remembering that we're a part of something grand and each of us is special just because we exist on this planet. So my friend, I ask you - are you part of the universe, or is the universe apart of you? **Jot down your thoughts:**

Consult the Stars: Take a moment to pull up your natal birth chart on a credible astrology website of your choice. Make note of your planetary placements and houses to help you to decode your unique cosmic blueprint.

In the space below, paste your chart or make notes for future reference.

THE 42 DIVINE PRINCIPLES OF MA'AT

At this point in time, and especially if you've been tuned into my YouTube Channel or attended a talk on the Wisdom App (@cortinajenelle) - many of you holding this book may have heard of at least a mention of Ma'at, which is synonymous with balance, justice, truth and fairness in many indigenous contexts. Whether you identify as someone who is Black, indigenous or not, there are great riches in Spirit and truth that can be gained by understanding what I like to call the universal principle of Ma'at, mother of ethics, balancer of karma and giver of a sense of right and wrong. As we just discussed in previous sections, there has long been a split between science and spirituality, but I pose the question of what we would gain by marrying the two together once again? Could that be a determining factor in our sense of ethics about what happens with the environment? It is hard to say for sure and the answer will be different for everyone. Yet, as far as I can tell what the principles of Ma'at (see reference on Kemetic culture) reinforce are a sense of awareness and equity in how we show up for our relationships to ourselves, each other and the wider planet. This isn't religion. This is science.

When I traveled to Egypt a few years ago, I listened to a lecture on the restoration of "Ma'at" to the planet. It won't be for everyone, but if it's something that resonates for you, I have a few key points to share as food for thought:

- The need for restoration (or to be in a state of bringing back) of Ma'at (as an energy) to the planet would mean the planet is currently imbalance in Truth, Balance, Justice, Righteousness and Morality.
- If there are still people in positions of power and our Ma'at (as an energy) on the planet is off, how do you even begin to talk to someone with higher "rank" than you about what it takes to restore it?
- How much longer can the planet go on in absence of Truth, Balance, Justice, Righteousness and Morality?

To be honest, my work with Ma'at on my spiritual path and further studies of these principles is one of the things that compelled me to write this book in the first place. For me doing nothing is not an option, and in my opinion, naction is STILL an action. Indecision is STILL a decision. Ma'at comes to remind us of these very same things. There is polarity and duality in all things created under the Sun. To achieve the balance, we have to see where we have been imbalanced. In life, part of our work is to how best achieve that balance and do our best to lighten our load - physically, mentally, emotionally and spiritually. Ma'at principles have shown me a way to reverse the sense of doom that there is nothing I can do to be of service in the world. Every small action is a big step. Ma'at comes to ask us - "is your heart as light as a feather?"

Have you ever read the Ten Commandments in the Holy Bible for example? If you're nodding yes then, you have essentially also heard of SOME of the Principles of Ma'at without even realizing it. The laws of Maat are believed to be dated back as far as 2925 BC, meaning they would pre-date the Ten Commandments in the Bible by 2000 years+. As I share all 42 Principles of Ma'at, I'm also leaving you some space to write your reflections in the margins. What does your faith, religion or belief have to say about principles of ethics? Are any similar to these? How is your life aligned with doing the "higher good"?

Keep in mind that this exercise is meant to get you thinking about what it would look like to live in a society where our mutually held codes of ethics were more front-facing, as a way to bring people together. What would shift in your life? What would stay the same? Who around you would change or stay the same?

- I have not committed sin.

- I have not committed robbery with violence.

- I have not stolen.

- I have not slain men or women.

- I have not stolen food.

- I have not swindled offerings.

- I have not stolen from God/Goddess.

- I have not told lies.

- I have not carried away food.

- I have not cursed.

- I have not closed my ears to truth.

- I have not committed adultery.

- I have not made anyone cry.

- I have not felt sorrow without reason.

- I have not assaulted anyone.

- I am not deceitful.

- I have not stolen anyone's land.

- I have not been an eavesdropper.

- I have not falsely accused anyone.

- I have not been angry without reason.

- I have not seduced anyone's wife.

- I have not polluted myself.

- I have not terrorized anyone.

- I have not disobeyed the Law.

- I have not been exclusively angry.

- I have not cursed God/Goddess.

- I have not behaved with violence.

- I have not caused disruption of peace.

- I have not acted hastily or without thought.

- I have not overstepped my boundaries of concern.

- I have not exaggerated my words when speaking.

- I have not worked evil.

- I have not used evil thoughts, words or deeds.

- I have not polluted the water.

- I have not spoken angrily or arrogantly.

- I have not cursed anyone in thought, word or deeds.

- I have not placed myself on a pedestal.

- I have not stolen what belongs to God/Goddess.

- I have not stolen from or disrespected the deceased.

- I have not taken food from a child.

- I have not acted with insolence.

- I have not destroyed property belonging to
  God/Goddess.

GATEKEEPERS: THE AFRICAN ROOTS OF LGBTQ

There is always deviation from what seems to be the "norm" as science shows us time and time again. Yet, for us humans, mainly having to do with control, there has been a massive overemphasis on masculinity these last several generations to say the least. Medicine has already proven that all humans have a composition of both estrogen and testosterone. On an energetic level, the presence (or absence) of these hormones influence our unique expression or blueprint and is what we call being "masculine" or "feminine". The manifestation of those energies in various, unique ways is what creates diversity (or divergence) in our ecosystem in the first place. Plants are cool with it, animals are fine with it and yet, our human nature is to grapple with what makes us beautiful. As a member of the LGBTQ community, this is a real pain and struggle that nearly took my life. I felt odd. I felt too "unacceptable". Until I started celebrating what made me unique and understood that it had everything to do with how "feminine" or "masculine" I was. I am me. We have all been subject to the fractures in cultures, spirituality and traditions that once not only welcomed the LGBTQ community but celebrated, revered and honored them as holders of great medicine, divine wisdom and spiritual gifts only privy to those who danced between the lines, if you will. Much of this history has been lost, but my work, research and studies has gained me access to deeper insights into what life was like in Black, indigenous cultures before the impact of colonization and imperialism spread globally. Although the information I share here may not be true for ALL cultures, I would go as far to say that for the lineages we represent, surely there is more to the story than man plus woman equals family, the end. Furthermore, knowing this aspect of my cultural history deeply transformed why + how I was doing collective liberation work and who with. For me, there is no place for religious dogma in changemaking work because we cannot heal the ancestral trauma or claim reparations until ALL of us are unchained. However, there is all the room for Spirit and in involving spirituality in activism work, we are moved from a place of inspired action as opposed to be the producer or consumer of emotional manipulation around social constructs we agreed a long time ago were not real. If a thing is truly not real, why do we pay it so much attention? Or maybe better questions are, if race is a socially and politically created construct, how do we get it out of our mouths?...if we were truly all created equal in the image of God, the Divine, Source, then why has the LGBTQ community been getting trampled on for so long? The short answer is what the answer will always be - power and control. The last layer I want to douse on this as food for thought is this - once I started layering my racial equity work with wellness work with spiritual studies work with economic development work with creativity work with environmental work, I realized that the true injustice, what colonization truly took from us was/is our connection with our divinity and our sacred connection to the planet. So, know thyself. If the research that I've shared so far hasn't already made the case for why we must go further back to go forward, let this excerpt from *The Spirit of Intimacy: Ancient Teachings in the Ways of Relationships* by (the late) Sobonfu Somé emphasize it:

The words "gay" and "lesbian" do not exist in the village, but there is the word "gatekeeper". Gatekeepers are people who live a life at the edge between two worlds -- the world of the village and the world of spirit...the gatekeepers stand on the threshold of the gender line. They are mediators between the two genders. They make sure that there is peace and balance between women and men...they simply play the role of "the sword of truth and integrity". Now what would happen if you're dealing with a culture that doesn't care about these gateways? What happens is that a gay person cannot do his or her job. Gatekeepers are left unable to accomplish their purpose. This is one of the most distinguishing factors about gays in the village...the life of gay people in the West is in many ways a reaction to pressure from a society that rejects them. This is partly because a culture that has forgotten so much about itself will displace certain groups of people, such as the gay community, from their true roles...gatekeepers are encouraged to fulfill the role they're born to, to use their gifts in the interests of the community."

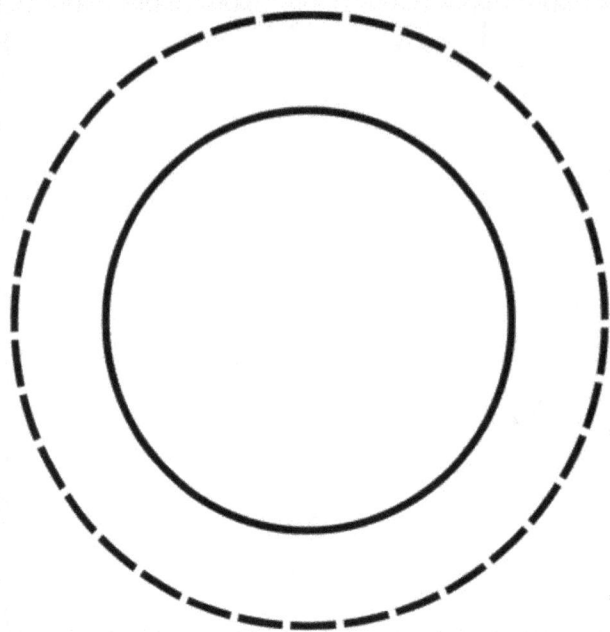

SHOOT FOR THE MOON

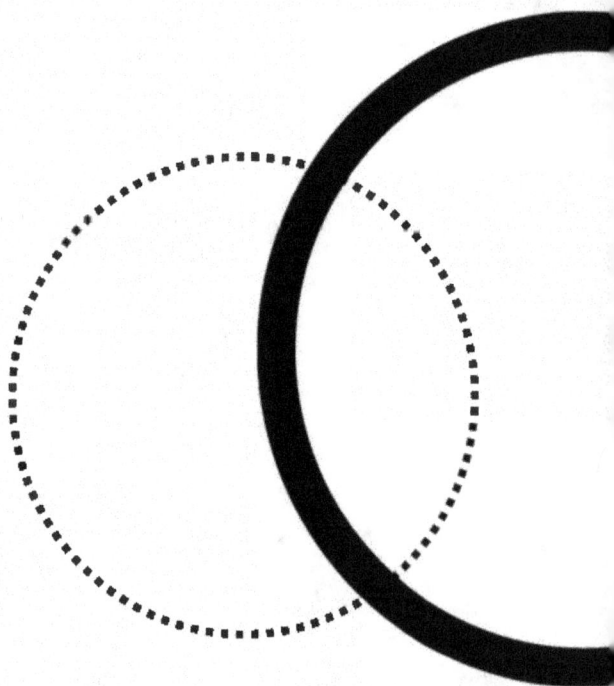

INTERVIEW YOUR INNER CHILD

As we sit in circle together, even though not in the same physical space, I want to name that this is a tender section of the book and may touch on some areas within yourself or your life that you have never reconciled or spent time with and wherever you are with this is okay. If you have said yes to showing up for yourself and the world by arriving at this page, then trust the process. As someone who has done a lot of spiritual, mental, emotional and physical healing over the last 20+ years, know that I empathize with you and stand with you. If you can, take a moment to light a candle each time you come to this section of the book and really invite the truth in that life IS a ceremony. If not a candle, maybe you pour libation, or use other natural tools shared in the "Nature's Apothecary" section of this book. As I write these words, more than anything I just want you to know you are not alone in your pain, in the struggle, or trying to make sugar from shit. Your story is my story. We all have our trials. And glory to the divinity in us all when we can find the buried treasures, share our story and find meaning in our lives. We first begin by going back to take the hand and reconcile the trust of our inner child.

In earlier chapters of this book, I have touched on sovereignty, authenticity and your divine birthright simply because of the majesty within you, all that created you and flows through you. I have often heard it said that we are closest to God as children...full of awe, wonder, an active imagination, a very thin veil between our physical realm and the spiritual one and infinite hope for what is possible. I was in dialogue with a beloved friend the other day and we were talking about the inner child work we do for ourselves and others and we arrived at the question many of us (adults) heard or were asked when we were younger "What do you want to be when you grow up?" As I reflected more on the exchange, thinking of my own experience, I realized that for many of us - therein lies the insert of our first deep wound. I don't know about you but when I was asked this question in elementary school, I had some very clear initial answers (which I don't mind saying were architect, being on stage, writing and helping people...no particular order) and the feedback I got when I shared those answers included "they don't make any money", "Black people don't do that", "why not being a doctor or lawyer or something, you're smart..." and laughter. So naturally, I thought the adults in my life would know because they were on the other side of the question so I abandoned those dreams and started pursuing being a pediatric nurse. With changes, twists, turns and interesting lessons along the way, here I am today doing EXACTLY what my inner child confessed lit her up - I'm an architect of businesses, brands, communities and systems; I'm a motivational speaker, MC, poet and artist who has taken the stage to help people more time than I can count; and the writing? You're holding proof of me making that dream a reality. No matter how long it took me to find my way back, I did. I deeply believe that in order for us to find lasting happiness and wholeness in our lives, we need the responsibilities of adulthood that give us something to build + honor in ADDITION to the childlike state that keeps us humble, adventurous, curious, playful and flexible. It's not an either or. It's a both and. I also believe that our inner child manifests as either our Higher Self (an inner child that has matured into the light) or our Shadow Self (an inner child that has been silenced and put in a dark corner), depending on the relationship we've built with ourselves, or how long we've been trying to keep up with what the world thinks we should be or do with our lives. I'll let you in on a secret that has taken me alot of soul searching, self help books, therapy and pain to find out - no one is in a better position to tell you what you want to be when you grow up than you. And maybe the question that we should actually be asking children in elementary school is "What did you come to bring into the world? What lights you up?" Ask that to a little human you know and watch their eyes light up as they tell you all the amazing things they can do. And practice your inner child work by believing them and giving them more of what THEY love. We are only borrowers of this planet from the generations after us and if we can't nurture childhood dreams or the inner child of another, we should probably just get out of the way. I'll touch more on this in this section later, but for now - you and your inner child have a special date. All you need to do is pick where, what time and bring these:

QUESTIONS FOR YOUR INNER CHILD:

- When have you felt the most fulfilled?
- When have you felt like you needed more love?
- Tell me about a time when you felt like a superhero?
- Tell me about a time when you felt sad, not supported or not listened to enough?
- What did you come to bring into the world?
- Tell me about something you had to figure out yourself that you feel really proud of yourself for?
- What lights you up?

Remember, this is for you and your inner child. There is no wrong way to do it if you're showing up. Some suggestions though would be to commit - put it on your calendar. Take yourself somewhere you loved as a kid, or as similar as you can find. Sit in silence, read the questions and journal. Or read them aloud and audio record what first comes to mind. Be gentle. Be open.

WHAT LIGHTS YOU UP?

Welcome home, SOL-journer. Just in case you haven't read the previous chapter on "Interview with Your Inner Child", I want to make the suggestion that you go back and read that, as well as take your inner child out on a play date before you dive into this chapter here. You will want that context before we go into this chapter here now, mostly for yourself so, consider the two a pair! Now, review the questions and your answers from your playdate with your inner child if you haven't already (not counting the day you captured the answers) and use that in the next page to fill in responses with the wisdom you have just gained. Remember the old adage "And a child shall lead them"? I deeply believe that is in reference to our inner child helping us find the way back to our truest selves so, congratulations on taking initial steps. For those who already have a relationship with the child inside, may this work forge a deeper bond with that bright-eyed, bushy-tailed version of you. It is also important at this point in to remember your support map and call in more hands from your village as you nurture this child albeit a therapist, coach, friends, Spirit or motivational content online. You are not alone.

Now that you are equipped with some important info, some tools, some extra hands, let's talk to the adult you:

WISDOM FROM YOUR INNER CHILD:

- What dots have started connecting for you?
- What things did you love doing that you have lost touch with? What caused you to put them away?
- What things seem to make you sad that brought up more sadness in you now? Does this need support?
- Where did you have a big grin on your face?
- What would you do regardless of getting paid?
- Where would you take you inner child out to play?
- How can you keep nurturing this relationship?

Ho'oponopono: an Ancient Hawai'ian Prayer

To My Inner Child,

I am sorry. Please forgive me. Thank you. I love you.

When it comes to letting go of karmic attachments, and energetic cords, **Ho'oponopono** works, as it clears and integrates the energy. It is a powerful forgiveness and letting go of the most challenging of life experiences. It is a balancing + co-ordinating vibration promoting both reconciliation and forgiveness. **Ho'oponopono** means 'to make right' – it brings balance to the self and all relationships, even with one's ancestors.

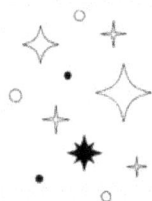

"If we can accept that we are the sum total of all past thoughts, emotions, words, deeds and actions and that our present lives and choices are colored or shaded by this memory bank of the past, then we begin to see how a process of correcting or setting aright can change our lives, our families and our society."

Morrnah Nalamaku Simeona

[a Hawai'ian Kahuna Lapa'au]

A WORD ON IDENTITY

Growing up, I was a "tomboy". Now, before you correct me let me share that this was in the late 80s, early 90s when there was little to no representation of the LGBTQ community anywhere that I could see. Not in my small rural mountain town in the South, not on television, not in the books I read but I apparently liked doing "boy" things so that was the label I was given. The truth was I liked playing with lego sets, video games, sports (especially football because I had a killer long throw) as much as I liked playing with dolls, make believe house, art, etc. For me, as with everything else about me, I didn't feel compelled to choose - we are complex beings in a multiverse might I remind you - except when everyone else around me starting reminded me that I needed to. So, I started looking around to all the women in my life and as much as I could see some things didn't make sense to me, the programming as insidious and tricky as it is, slipped in anyway to cope with the initiation of childhood. Most of the women around me were Black single mothers that seemed to have a inferiority complex with men and a love-hate relationship about being a woman so I was getting very mixed cues about which side was for me. As I moved away to college and into early adulthood, my Queerness was ready to be lived out loud which added even more layers to the complexity of whether I was a boy or girl because I truly felt like both. Reading books like *Coming Out, Coming Alive* by Grace Lawson; *Same Sex in the City* by Lauren Blitzer & Lauren Levin and my first therapist, who was an Apache shaman and licensed psychiatrist, introducing me to what being queer (or modernly called Two-Spirit) meant in Native American spirituality completely blew me open in the best of ways. Since that time of course it hasn't all been rainbows and gumdrops (or, maybe it actually has involved ALOT of rainbows, ha!) but on this side I know that I am better for it. When I think about babies from the rural south like me that have even more room to INTRODUCE the world to who they are as opposed to the world sliding them into a box, I am moved to tears. Even as "young" as I am, I did not have that privilege. In my lifetime, which is far from over, I have witnessed shifts in epic proportions around freeing love, unboxing our gender identities and being called what honors us. It gives me hope and pride everyday because I know my people and I did our part and we stand on the shoulders of so many greats who marched, protested, fashioned and organized their way to the justice of today. As we move into talking about the divine feminine and divine masculine, I just wanted to pause and share a bit of my truth in this way. And as I have come to find out in my work, there has always been purpose and greatness for those who dance between the genders and I'm here for it (more in "Gatekeepers"). I'm honored to be all of me.

DIVINE FEMININE +
DIVINE MASCULINE

As we approach this topic, I first want to be clear - when we speak about the Divine Feminine and Divine Masculine energies, try not to think about that man or woman you know, try not to think about all the ways you have perhaps seen those who are "masc" or "femme" behave or operate in society. When we speak of the Divine Feminine and Divine Masculine, we are speaking of energies that we ALL contain. In the "Gatekeepers" chapter of this book, you may remember me referring to the feminine and the masculine energy that we all have. Everything we experience here on the planet contains the duality of an inward, receptive motion (which science considers feminine) and an outward, external motion (which science considers masculine). Let's go a little deeper then. Have you ever tried to take in alot of air and hold your breath without exhaling? It doesn't last long, does it? Have you ever seen a building with only exits and no entrances? These are simple examples to make the point of duality exists in many forms in our daily lives, whether we've been noticing it or not. Duality is how we measure balance and imbalance is what creates space for disease or *dis*-ease meaning a block to natural flow.

And let's take it even a level deeper now. How does your body feel when you're just on go mode all the time with no play, no rest, no sleep, no relaxation? It can't sustain itself for very long can it? That is because the energetics surrounding your body is imbalanced. The external action of doing things out in the world has to be meet with the internal action of just BE-ing, playing, allowing yourself to be nurtured or following your bliss. Sounding familiar? Over the last 5 years especially talk about self-care has been trending and amazing organizations like The Nap Ministry remind us that rest is restorative justice just as much as organizing change makers. Self-care is now in our collective consciousness because we have been operating in a masculine-driven war of external action, productivity, efficiency and martyrdom by any means necessary. The planet and our collective heart is asking us to recalibrate and come back into balance with ourselves and if we have to see self-care memes and apps that remind us to meditate to get there, so be it. What I don't hear enough people talking about though is what is actually taking place for us all on a cellular and collective level - this is a MAJOR shift that we are in the midst of. You've probably felt some growing pains around it and had to make many adjustments to how you're spending your time to not overwork or neglect yourself, your family, home or heart-centered priorities. And to be honest, that's exactly where we want to be if we are going to heal the planet from wherever we are. The divine feminine is rising, awakening from her slumber on the planet, within us, in how we work and how we show up in the world and it's beautiful to behold.

[LETTER TO THOSE ON A] SOJOURN OF LIGHT

Dear Starseed,

You are here to birth a new world.
You are here to birth a new reality.
You are here to birth a new possibility.
You are pioneer on the forefront of your Consciousness.
Do not expect to "belong".
Do not expect to be "validated" or get approval.
Do not expect anyone to give you permission.
In fact, they will not and you must show up anyway.
Do not expect anyone to bestow anything upon you.
You are a Sovereign, Magician, Warrior and Lover.
You are the one that bestows and creates belonging for
yourself. Move towards your open doors.
Claim your crown.
Claim your throne.
Create your empire.
Create spaces where you can live, dance, breathe, play
and be. Abundance is your birthright.
No one is going to hand anything to you.
No one is coming to save you.
The time is now to be the hero in your own story.

[original poetry by]

Cortina Jenelle Caldwell

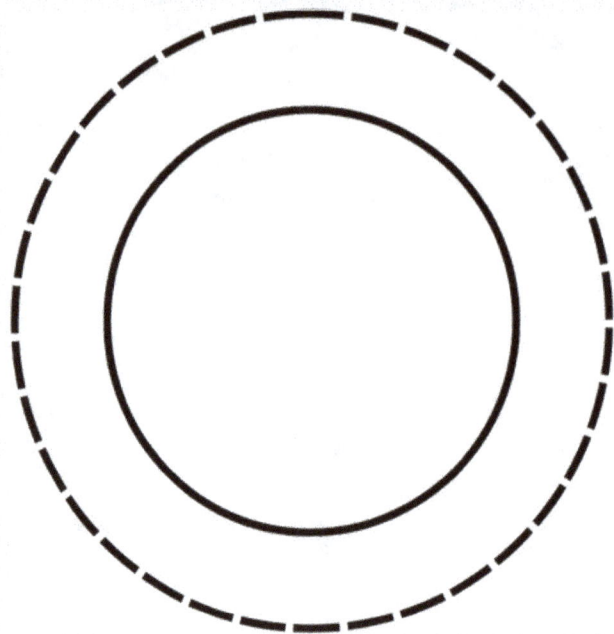

LETTING GO

SHADOW WORK AS ANCESTRAL HEALING

Over the past two years, I have heard more people speaking about their ancestral connections or the work they feel called to do around ancestral healing than any other time in my life. How about you? With all that I just named about the rebalancing of Divine Feminine energy as well as the LGBTQ community taking its rightful place as gatekeepers once again, you might see why our ancestors are real busy these days, compelling us to dig deep and do the inner work so that we bring that justice into and through our family lines. There is much that is imbalanced on Gaia and the heartbreaking truth is that it has been at the hands of (hu)mankind so it is our responsibility to clean up our mess. Do you go into your grandmother's house, spill some oil or juice on the floor and just walk away and leave it there? My guess is...no. You wouldn't. So why are we (as a collective) so comfortable leaving our mess for someone else to clean up on the planet? Whether you have children of your own or not, I urge you to think of them if you are one to spill and split (metaphorically). It is on their backs that you are placing what was originally yours to do here now.

So, as it is with shadow work. To explain the concept in general terms, from my perspective, it comes down to two things - the necessity of shadow work comes about because of a silenced or wounded inner child; and/or the necessity of shadow work comes about because someone in our family (ancestral) line left unfinished, unresolved work that we must now pick up...which is still most likely because of *their* silenced or wounded inner child. Your Shadow Self (or shadow) then, is the darkness within you and your Higher Self is the light within you - we all contain this duality - and our responsibility as human beings with Spirit consciousness is to learn temperance, or balance between the two. Through my lived experience and reading of some great books such as *Feeding Your Demons: Ancient Wisdom for Resolving Inner Conflict* by Tsultrim Allione and *Shadow Work* by Kyree Anthony what I know for sure is that our Shadow Self is just as much of a teacher as the more popular, Higher Self. There is alot that we can learn by going into the darkness and understanding how we got stuck there, why the wound won't heal, and how we can make shifts moving forward for the benefit of ourselves, our families, society, the planet and most certainly, our ancestors. If your goal in life is to reach enlightenment or you know you are on a hero(ine)'s journey, let me be the first to point out that no superhero movie I've seen yet has showed a metahuman that did not first have to face their fears to achieve inner mastery and unlock their full potential. What were they up to? Shadow work. Who was the one holding them back? Themselves. Moral of it all?

You are the hero of your own story. You have the power within you to unlock your divinity, sovereignty and creative authority in your life. No one can do your Shadow Work for you. You can choose not to do it, but it will just keep getting passed around the family like a hot potato until someone finally says yes. When and if you do, know that you're not alone. Getting crowned as the royalty you are will require you to journey through the underworld first. It is not light work, I will not lie to you. Will it be worth it, you ask? What would make it worth it to you? I would encourage you to make a list here and now, if you haven't wanted to face your fears, or heal unhealthy family patterns, or make a connection with your ancestors, what would make doing the work worth it to you? Then when you're ready, ask your Shadow Self to join you in circle to share answers to these questions:

- When are all the times I felt like a bad person?
- When are all the times I felt wronged? By who?
- What family legacy do I want to end with me? Why?
- What does that external admiration show me about myself? Or what limitations I put on myself?
- What family traditions do I want to carry forward?
- What questions do I have about myself?
- What are positive things I wish others would do?
- What will I a) gain and b) lose by integrating my Shadow Self? (i.e. being my own source of light, having boundaries)

On a final note, let me be the first to remind you that there is honor in being tapped to clear the family line. It will be hard, it will require strength but it will absolutely be worth it, whether you see shift in your lifetime or not.

FALSE EVIDENCE
APPEARING REAL
[F.E.A.R.]

As you're doing work with your Shadow Self, Higher Self and the inner child, the inner critic (or saboteur) is going to be just a busy to remind you of all the reasons why what you're trying and what you're up to will NOT work. Let me say this part loud for the people in the back - **EVERYTHING the saboteur/inner critic says is a LIE.** So instead, hear my voice (in your voice) as I say to you that:

You are on the journey of the hero(ine). You had to leave comfort in order to go about life in your unique way. You failed the first time. So what? You needed to learn where your energetic containers were loose in order to go back in and install all of the boundaries needed. You went out to conquer your limitations again, and this time YOU win. Out of the ashes, rise like a golden Sun. Life is about discovery. You never failed at life. You failed to let others tell you how to live yours. LET GO. Let go of fears of being judged or disowned. Your energetic shields must be strong to deal with the bigness of you. It is up to you to see this through, and no one else. No one needs to have your back. You have your own back. Good vibes attract good tribes. So, journey. Live. The Earth is your witness.

- Give up your vows of silence which only serve to protect the old and stale.
- Unwind your vigilance, soften your belly, open your jaw and speak the truth you long to hear.
- Be the champion of your right to be here.
- Know that you must accept your rejected qualities, adopting them with the totality of your love and commitment. Aspire to let them never feel outside of love again.
- Venerate your too-muchness with an enduring vow to become increasingly weird and eccentric.
- Send out signals of originality with frequency and constancy, honoring whatever small trickle of response you get until you reach a momentum.
- Notice your helpers and not your unbelievers.
- Remember that your offering needs no explanation. It is its own explanation.
- Go it alone until you are alone with others. Support each other without hesitation.
- Become a crack in the network that undermines the great towers of establishment.
- Make your life a wayfinding, proof that we can live outside the usual grooves.
- Brag about your escape.
- Send your missives into the network to be reproduced. Let your symbols be adopted + adapted + transmitted broadly into the new culture we're building together.

The Black Sheep Gospel

[Belonging: Remembering Ourselves Home (c) Toko-pa Turner, 2017]

TRIGGERED TO TREASURED

In true form as we're talking about feeling and healing, there must be a conversation about triggers. Back in my early days with Creative Facilitation work, I was introduced to the framework of Comfort, Stretch, Panic (for a walkthrough on how to implement this in a meeting or group space, checkout "Toolkit: Decolonize Your Meetings" towards the back). What I loved about Comfort, Stretch, Panic is that it gave us a completely different approach to talking through triggers. Let's be real - someone was often feeling triggered in the spaces I was working in in those days because we were just on the precipice of pronoun usage and not nearly enough people had begun doing their personal anti-Blackness, anti-oppression work so everything we brought up had the potential for being triggering. As a participant in spaces, I witnessed entire agendas and meetings get derailed because the proper thing to do seemed to be to stop and make space for the person feeling triggered. As our work, and we all evolved Comfort, Stretch, Panic was an amazing tool to allow the person feeling triggered to name that and express to the group where they were at simply and then take accountability for re-calibrating.

Now, I am in no way saying that triggers are bad. From my perspective, triggers are teachers that show us where our wounds are. What I AM saying and hope to make clear to you is this - to ask that everyone else in a space around you pause and sit with you while you process the fact that someone poked an invisible wound they didn't know was there is not going to heal the wound. Only YOU can do that. When you have a scab, what things do you need to let it heal? Think about it. This brings me back around to much of what we discussed in "Shadow Work as Ancestral Healing". The only way a wound could still be opened is if it hasn't gotten the medicine or air it needs to heal. So when we are triggered, it's actually us feeling in our bodies that something needs our attention. If someone is intentionally triggering you after you've already named your version of "Ouch.", then it may be time to put some boundaries in place which we'll touch on in a few chapters. To support your move from triggered to treasured, here are a few power statements:

- May the healing I achieve not only benefit me, but ALL sentient beings. May it benefit all in our orbit.
- I can show up as I am, allowing people to see my process. I offer myself compassion and loving kindness so that I may offer this to others.
- I trust my intuition in order to stay in alignment with my Higher Self and reduce my own suffering.
- No matter what is in the way of my healing. Bless the way. Bless these teachers that show up on my path.
- I vow loyalty to my light and to live by the light.

YOUR RULES OF ENGAGEMENT

Being treasured by others begins with treasuring yourself and once you treasure yourself, you can treasure Pachamama and all her bounty. Another big aspect of this work is to know yourself well enough to establish your rules of engagement. What do you stand for? What are you unwilling to stay silent about? Take a moment now to write these questions down somewhere where you take notes, or record audio if that works better for you. I encourage you to make this a family activity with children or your partner if you feel open to do so. It can be a great way to identify what you, and those you love, value on a deep level. If and when something matters to you, you do whatever is necessary to protect, honor and preserve it. At some point in our human evolution, I would love to see the day when we are taught to honor and fight for the planet as much as we are romantic love. Can you imagine if the world was less involved in our love lives and more involved in building inclusive ecosystems? Obviously, we're not there yet but I draw that example to show that we can trace action to value and value to money/attention. Having clear values and rules of engagement teaches others how to treat you, or not.

As you begin to think about what these are for you, you might choose to adopt some from the list in "42 Divine Principles of Ma'at" or come up with some of your own. As you are making your list of rules of engagement, I would encourage you to start with one list for your overall stance, then move to building a list for work (especially if you're responsible for hiring/recruiting!), a work for home life (with input from all), and a list for your friendships or partnerships. Do not, however, just let these lists collect dust. Love yourself enough and love what you're building in the world enough to hold yourself and others accountable to these. Trust that when they are crossed, it is data for you that there may not be alignment. It doesn't mean they are a bad person, it means you know what you deserve and you mean it.

Some food for thought as you uphold your rules/values:
- Expectations are clear for you and others.
- Everyone is aligned and on the same page.
- There is clarity and transparency.
- Craft clear, direct communication.
- (On the job) The hiring of others is not the place for people pleasing. Leave that for social hour. You have an empire to build and/or run.
- Set clear boundaries. When these are violated, do not take it personally. See violations as data points of where you need to fill in leaks in your energetic containers and take appropriate action.
- Check character of a person not what they present.

BOUNDARIES ARE GIFTS, NOT BARRIERS

How are you feeling, beloved? If you are feeling nervous about having to assert yourself if you never have, or learning to speak up when something goes against your values, or having to learn to communicate directly - I get it. And I see you. This was not second nature for me initially for me, either. I grew up in a household and family where children were expected to be seen, not heard and silence was the solution to all the problems. I had to unlearn that programming not just to make it where I wanted to go in life, but because the silence eventually turned on ME. My dance with learning to put in boundaries for myself has been a spiral dance and sometimes it was one step forward and two steps back. Every DAY, I have to uphold my rules of engagement and it's not always comfortable or easy. I have to check myself every day on moments when it feels easier to give in to someone's small request of my time when I've made plans for myself, or allow a disruption when I've made it clear verbally or nonverbally that I was in work mode. I have learned over time that if I choose to ignore my intuition or go against my commitments to myself and my rules of engagement, it always costs me. ALWAYS.

Instead of letting that illusion of F.E.A.R. creep back in, what I would like to suggest is a bit of a reframe around boundaries. Boundaries are gifts, NOT barriers. Boundaries are one of the deepest acts of self-love, self-care, self-worth and self-concept we could display to communicate to ourselves (i.e. inner child, Higher Self) that we can be trusted and that we do matter. All throughout childhood and school, our boundaries are crossed in ways that we do not even consciously recognize. The list is way too long for me to go into here, but as an adult (or whatever age you are as you read this!) you owe it to yourself to protect the treasure that is you. You are sacred and you are here on purpose, remember? Your body is a temple. Your mind is brilliant. Your Spirit is divine. What reason can you think of to NOT make sure people who access you physically, spiritually, emotionally or mentally have your permission to do so? Boundaries, in my perspective, are inherently connected to consent. Consent is absolutely something we should be all learning about from as young as we can speak and alot of parents these days are finding ways to bring that into conscious parenting. Yet, we still have so much further to go as a collective so that those vulnerable to experiencing violent acts of boundary crossing feel empowered and able to speak up before things go too far...or at least to notice the red flags and to call in support when someone repeatedly crosses a boundary. So with all of this said, if you felt hung up about making your rules of engagement or enforcing your boundaries, let me give you permission to let that shit GO. You deserve the best and you should expect it in return.

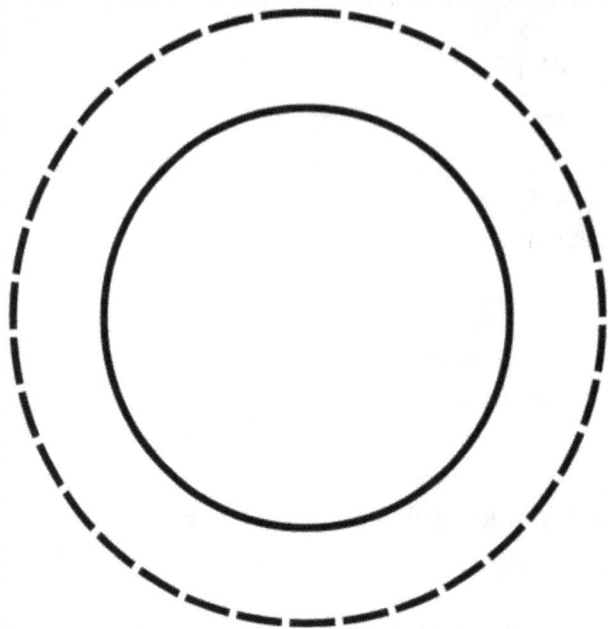

LOVE YOUR (PACHA)MAMA

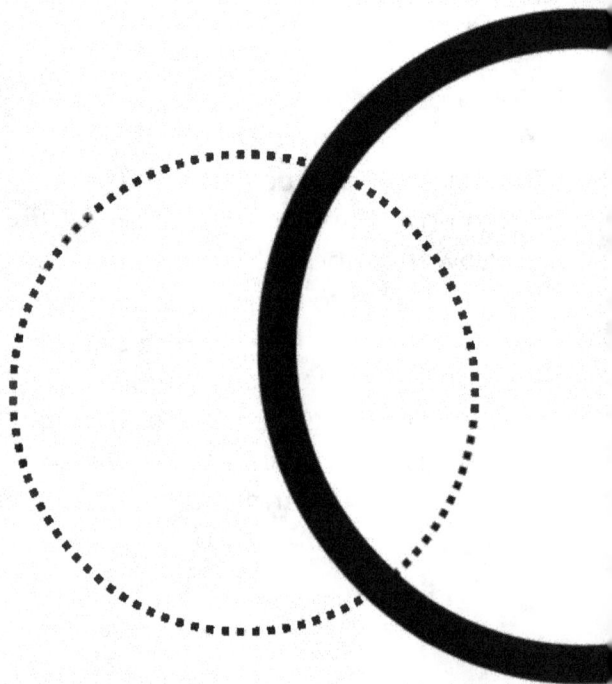

ANCIENT EARTH WISDOM
+ COSMIC GUIDANCE

If you have ever been in space with me or listened to one of my talks, you may have heard me refer to collective liberation in the same sentence that I'm talking about ancestral healing and creative entrepreneurship. Why? From my perspective, lived experience and education (formal and experiential) these things ARE inherently connected. So as we begin to shift our attention from internal work to external work in the second half of this book, this chapter felt like an especially important marker and bridge for how we put it all into practice. And for those who read the earlier chapter on "Divine Feminine + Divine Masculine" you will probably recognize this as the chapter that moves us from inhale to exhale...or from reflection to action. To make sure we are all on the same page, let's start with some definitions. When I refer to ancient Earth wisdom, I am speaking about the traditions and lifestyle practiced by those (indigenous) who came before to live in *harmony with* Gaia. And if you look around you hard enough, you'll see that it is still very much present in our day to day life - the Farmer's Almanac, zodiac charts, permaculture - these are all examples of how the ancient Earth wisdom have never left our side. It's just time we acknowledged them.

This list is short and there are many other ways and examples of how Ancient Earth wisdom has been passed down through generations over time. There was a time when Earth was referred to as the Divine Mother and evolved to garner the title "Mother Earth" by those who took to studying her rhythms, cycles, seasons or working her land. As children born of her, there was a certain respect and sacredness in the way cultures across the globe chose to live and function to keep her centered in all things. With patriarchy, capitalism and colonization, we lost that sacred connection just as we lost our lands.

Have you ever noticed your natural inclination to look upwards toward the sky when you're thinking about something or asked a question? Why might that be? Of course, not everyone's answer will be the same, but I like to believe the guidance, protection and "voice" of authority is something in our collective consciousness. Cosmic guidance, then, is the reference to the "above". The stars, the planets, the galaxy and the universe. As named earlier chapters, astronomy and astrology have both proven that there is an energetic influence from other planets at certain celestial events. I wonder then, what kind of influence Earth, in her imbalanced state, is having on those other planets? In ancient Kemetic culture, the Netjer expressed as Nut (*noot*) was a Feminine energy whose body held the stars, galaxy and cosmos into balance as the Sun and Moon passed through her daily + infinitely. So when I speak of cosmic guidance, it's that guiding light, firm hand to hold and definitive action that helps to shape our path. Together, ancient Earth wisdom + cosmic guidance are the divine alignment and balanced action and reflection we need.

GRIEF IS THE COST
OF KNOWING LOVE

The grief about what has been lost is palpable. And truth be told, it can also get uncomfortable. For many of us, we have experienced untapped levels of grief since March 2020. Whether it was because a loved one transitioned, a lay off from a job, changes with school, shifting to being at home brought up buried feelings around our dreams, what (or who) we love and our relationship with time. All of it is valid and none of it needs validation from others for you to have permission to grieve. If you want more support making sense of nagging feelings in the back of your mind, I invite you to give my podcast, *Sojourn of Light*, particularly the episode, "Grief + Hope as Social Activism" may be supportive at this time. Grief is something that I have experienced many times in my life whether it was going away to college, the sudden loss of my biological father, pets who died, romantic breakups or even grief about decisions I felt I HAD to make to honor myself and my truest alignment. I had to grieve all of it. From my perspective, grief is evidence that we have loved, that we are alive and that we can still feel. I would be more worried if you DIDN'T grieve because it's a very human thing to do. Since it's not going anywhere anytime soon, let's touch on how we co-exist with grief.

77

Grief requires you to be willing to change and let go. And as much as its timing is often inconvenient, it's one of those "deal with it now, or *really* deal with it later" type situations. It is not easy to move through. But there is support and you have every right to take up space as you take care of yourself. In fact, let me just come out and say it - you are your greatest responsibility. Nature is the greatest cure-all there is, thankfully. Most any ailment or ill you could name, I can respond and say "there's a plant for that". Since we're limited on time and space here, I can only share a few, but grief support alone deserves its own standalone book. For more on this, check out the resource list for the book for more on the stages of grief. In my life, I've called on medical professionals, therapists, coaches, mentors, herbalists, movement, bodywork and plants to move my grief. Make good use of your support map to tap into resources right around you. For now, remember that grief is a very human thing to do and we can get to the other side of change with our hearts open.

PLANTS + HERBS* | Useful for teas, soaking baths, oils, salves:

☐ Lavender   ☐ Sage   ☐ Calendula
☐ Chamomile   ☐ Rosemary   ☐ Goldenrod
☐ Mullein   ☐ Holy Basil   ☐ Mint

MINERALS + CRYSTALS | Useful to carry or place in your space:
☐ Rose Quartz (unconditional love + peace)
☐ Amethyst (calms the nervous system + anxiety)
☐ Apache Tear (absorbs + releases grief)

Always check with a medical professional about your allergies or contraindications before consuming any herbs.

SOUND MEDICINE

Another powerful tool that has helped me personally with grief, trauma and healing has been sound. One of the things that I love most about sound medicine is that it is one of safest, most accessible tools for healing on the planet and the millions of people that gather globally in community to share music, attend festivals or concerts is evidence of that. In indigenous cultures sound was used by the ancients to invoke trance states during ceremony in order to speak with the Divine, mark rites of passage, communicate messages quickly to the village and support healing in many ways using instruments, rhythmic beats, chants and song. We just recently retained the right to play the drum publicly without it being considered "witchcraft" after it was banned and outlawed during the Trans-Atlantic slave trade. Fast forward to today, science has proven that our brain releases endorphins and lower our stress levels, especially when played at certain MegaHertz (or sound waves). Us being less-stressed out is certainly good for the planet in my book and if you want some guidance, I recommend adding *Woke Nation, Healing Meditation, Meditative Mind, Sound Forest, Relaxed Things* and *Taos Winds Spirit Music* to your YouTube channel list for peace and stress release. Or some jazz or classical wouldn't hurt!

OTHER LOVE NOTES

With the state of things in the world, I also want to name
that there are many other reasons we may turn to
nature for relaxation, release, grounding and healing
that we cannot do on our own. Some of you may choose
to turn to nature as opposed to inviting in more people
to help you. Some of you may use both. Either way is all
good. The most important thing to me is that you know
you have options and Pachamama has always been
providing for us the things we need in great bounty. To
me, this is all the more reason to care for this sacred
home we are borrowing for a short time...it feels selfish to
me to use up resources to the point of none being left for
anyone else. Have you ever sat down to a meal with
someone who took more than their share of food, not
leaving enough to go around? Even if you haven't, take a
moment to imagine that scenario. Chances are that
person would get the side eye by a few people from
around the table. Yet that is exactly what we're doing
when we turn our backs on the damage being done to
the water, land, mountains, forests and all the plants,
herbs, animals, crystals and MEDICINE available to us in
the process. If we lack, it's not because we did not have.

Here are a few ideas to invite in Nature's medicine more:

- Drink more water! Did you know that water is a crystalline substance that you can program with your intentions and it will follow? Did you know that we can survive longer with no food than we can with no water? Do your research on this to confirm for yourself but trust me when I say water is sacred.
- **Go for a walk outside.** Consider visiting a park, nature preserve, beach, lake or wherever calls to you.
- **Get barefoot.** Take time to feel Earth supporting you.
- **Take a workshop by a trusted community herbalist.**
- Download apps like PictureThis, PlantSnap or PlantNet (no affiliation to me, I just enjoy them!) and take your inner child or children on a scavenger hunt around the backyard or your favorite park. Be curious and find out what nature is growing under your nose!
- **Add some ideas of your own that you enjoy:**

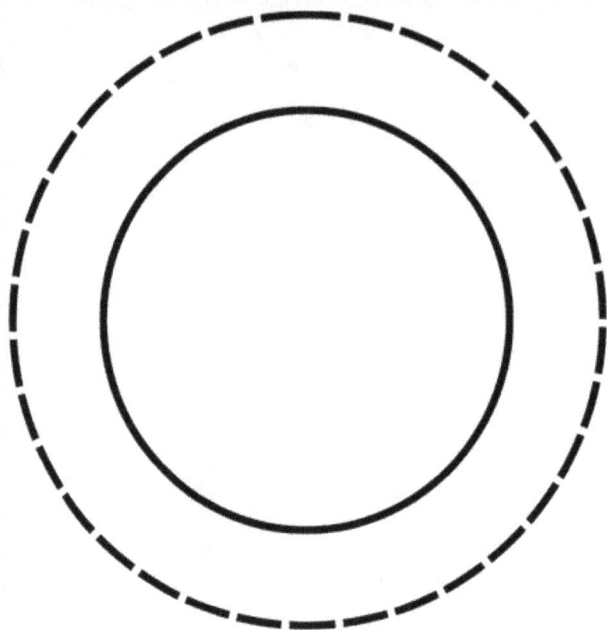

REDUCE WASTE,
REDUCE HARM

LEAVE NO TRACE

Do you feel the bigness you are apart of yet? I know I do. Throughout my travels around the world (10 countries so far, and counting!) and all over the lands occupied by the United States of America, I have seen many consistent truths and patterns. The more in touch with Mother Earth as our Divine Mother, provider of bountiful resources, that we are the more care, respect and honor that is put into how people live, work + build systems. The less in touch with Mother Earth we are, the more litter, waste, overconsumption, poisoned water, mistreatment of animals and pollution there is in how people live, work + build systems. Once this became clear for me, I had to do a complete and total shift to how I was approaching collective liberation, ancestral healing and creative entrepreneurship work. Once I saw the truth, I could not unsee it, and I hope the same is happening for you now. I have spoken in earlier chapters about the root cause of the problems that plague humanity being the same and all tracing back to the consequences and symptoms of dis-ease and imbalance brought forth by colonization. Just as nature exhibits a beautiful example of coexistence beyond difference, we too must learn that.

Rather than rattle off a bunch of facts and data points with historical timelines about how we got here, I instead want to emphasize a sense of urgency around us moving with inspired action to unravel what has us bound to convenience, consumption and disconnection. Each of these things costs us something. Even if you buy a cheap microwavable meal and it saves you money and time, it is costing you your health. Even if you buy produce in a grocery store, it is costing you connection with the land (or at least the farmer who tends and cares for the land). Even if you pay someone to come pick up your trash and recycling, it costs you knowing where your waste ends up. I mean really, have you ever researched the heart-breaking truth about recycling? Unless there is a working center processing the recycling, most of it STILL ends up in a landfill. And let's not even talk about the disrespect of dumping our trash on other countries, literally. As calm as I sound, this subject more than any other is deeply disturbing to me because many of us are turning a blind eye to how we're contributing to the climate crisis simply in our day-to-day decisions. If we each made intentional shifts, organized litter cleanup in our communities, created community art projects with old plastics, or only bought from humane, non-GMO, fair trade companies can you imagine how much would change? A lot. This is a conversation that I'm not hearing in environmental justice or climate change circles and I'm unapologetically here to bring it. There is no time to waste. Literally. And it is my generation and those after us that will be left to clean up the mess being made of the planet now. So, engage youth, engage creatives, hold businesses accountable and let's start BEING about waste reduction.

In my global and domestic travels, I have been heart broken to see the amount of litter on sidewalks, in sacred forests, on lands and just all around where people live. It's one thing to see it, and it's another thing to see people go on living, walk right by it and do nothing. It wrecks me. To move into action around this, there are a couple of things I'm already up to as part of the work of House of SOLEIL. One is this very book you're holding! 100% of proceeds from this book goes back into our pool of funds for Earth service work which has a focus on waste reduction, litter cleanup and creative re-use of plastics. It's a big undertaking for a global problem, but you can help by helping to spread the word about this book, gifting the book to those you love or making a direct donation. In fact, some of the early supporters of this book and this planetary work made it possible to plant seeds, support various farm(s) and furthering the wave. The long-term vision is for global green teams to have community hubs where we're tackling Earth service together, and creatively. We will need all hands on deck from engineers, to herbalists, to entrepreneurs, artists and everyone in between. Reach out if there's more you'd like to do to help. The other way we're acting is to share and spread the principles of Leave No Trace™ Seven Principles as founded by the Center for Outdoor Ethics:

- Stick to Trails
- Leave It As You Find It
- Keep Wildfire Wild
- Know Before You Go
- Trash Your Trash
- Be Careful With Fire
- Share the Trails

HEALING THE MOTHER WOUND

As someone who has my own challenges in relationship with the mother who birthed me, I have often been in support circles and community spaces where other folks are speaking of the pain of not having the kind of mother they hoped for. Stories of betrayal, abandonment, neglect, abuse are all too common. Speaking of maternal interconnectedness, I have spoken in earlier chapters about our beloved planet as the Divine Mother. As I have done my own healing work around my mama issues something that has been deeply helpful for me in addition to re-parenting myself has been falling into the arms of Mother Earth as the mother I had been yearning for for so long. During my time out in nature, I'm often asking - what can I learn and how can I contribute? From the medicine to my physical wounds, to the release of grief through my bare feet or nude body, to the resources available to build home, experience joy, explore my curiosities and follow my dreams - it has healed me. I offer this brief chapter and my truth to support anyone who has this mother wound. Many of our mothers did the best they could in a world that sought to divide and conquer the family unit so while we have every right to hold boundaries, remember they needed a mother too.

RETURNING TO
OUR ROOTS

This moment humanity is going through can now be
seen as a portal and as a hole. The decision to fall into the
hole or go through the portal is up to you. If they repent
of the problem and consume the news 24 hours a day,
with little energy, nervous all the time, with pessimism,
they will fall into the hole. But if you take this opportunity
to look at yourself, rethink life and death, take care of
yourself and others, you will cross the portal. Take care of
your home, take care of your body. Connect with the
middle body of your spiritual House. Connect to the
egregor [thought form or collective group mind] of your
spiritual home. Body, house, medium body, spiritual
house, all this is synonymous, that is to say the same.
When you are taking care of one, you are taking care of
everything else. Do not lose the spiritual dimension of
this crisis, have the aspect of the eagle, which from
above, sees the whole, sees more widely. There is a social
demand in this crisis, but there is also a spiritual demand.
The two go hand in hand. Without the social dimension,
we fall into fanaticism. But without the spiritual
dimension, we fall into pessimism and lack of meaning.
You were prepared to go through this crisis.

Take your toolbox and use all the tools at your disposal. Learn about resistance with indigenous and African peoples: we have always been and continue to be exterminated. But we still haven't stopped singing, dancing, lighting a fire and having fun. Don't feel guilty about being happy during this difficult time. You don't help at all by being sad and without energy. It helps if good things emanate from the Universe now. It is through joy that one resists. Also, when the storm passes, you will be very important in the reconstruction of this new world. You need to be well and strong. And, for that, there is no other way than to maintain a beautiful, happy and bright vibration. This has nothing to do with alienation. This is a resistance strategy. In shamanism, there is a rite of passage called the quest for vision. You spend a few days alone in the forest, without water, without food, without protection. When you go through this portal, you get a new vision of the world, because you have faced your fears, your difficulties ... This is what is asked of you. Let them take advantage of this time to perform their vision seeking rituals. What world do you want to build for yourself? For now, this is what you can do: serenity in the storm. Calm down and pray. Everyday. Establish a routine to meet the sacred every day. Good things emanate, what you emanate now is the most important thing. And sing, dance, resist through art, joy, faith and love.

Message from White Eagle, Hopi indigenous

[to the people | March 16, 2020]

EARTH SERVICE

Back when the Sun was still weak and the world was still in its pre-dawn phase, the first seed nestled deep within the Earth began to fight its way to the surface. The tiny seed could feel the warmth of the pre-dawn and wanted to push beyond its imprisonment within the Earth to see what was creating this wonderful warmth it had never felt before. The little seed began to grow large roots to stabilize itself for its journey upwards. The seed continued to slowly push its way forth, the other seeds were watching in amazement. Never before in their darkness had any other seed wanted to push upward to see where the new warmth was coming from. As the little seed emerged from the Earth, it became a small but strong stem. Then as it was no longer restricted by the soil, in the Earth, it spread its wings and grew leaves. The stem told the other seeds about this journey and growth above the soil and the other seeds were so excited about the prospect of the adventure, they decided they too wanted to grow and have new experiences. So over the next thousands of years, many other seeds found the courage and became brave, covering the world with leaves, bushes and flowers. Most importantly, creating a new environment for animals and insects to be born into.

Laura Bowen

"Sacred Beginnings" | Dreamtime Reading Cards

###

This parable came across my path in my writing process and it felt like it was divinely placed on my path for this chapter. Similar to the story of the caterpillar who must willingly enter darkness, turn into goo (nothingness) in order to fully experience a metamorphosis and emerge on the otherside with the strength and gentleness of a butterfly - the stories remind us that in order to change our reality and influence our environment, we MUST be willing to push through the darkness. The courage it took for that first seed is no different than the courage it takes a caterpillar to surrender to the unknown or the courage that will be required of you to do the inner work, Shadow work and inner child reconciliation. What is on the other side is uncertain, yes. But what if it's beautiful? And exactly what the world needed to evolve. I encourage you in this moment to stay encouraged. "What doesn't kill you only makes you stronger" may not be my favorite quote of all time but I do have to admit that there are times when the medicine is bitter. After you've gone at it alone, trust that you will not be alone forever. Whatever action is calling to you now to be brave and to show up even if you will stand out, may be the very thing that's needed so that those who ARE like you can FIND you. Use your discretion, of course, about how to move about the darkness. Know that courage leads to cooperation.

COOPERATION OVER CAPITALISM

In the chapter "Nguzo Saba", you may recall my overview of the seven core principles of Kwanzaa, which originated from African traditions in community. So let's look at the symbiosis between what's old (tradition) + new (coops):
- Open membership | Kujichagulia - Self-Determination
- Democratic control | Nia - Purpose
- Economic participation | Ujamaa - Coop Economics
- Independence | Kuumba - Creativity
- Education + Training | Ujima - Collective Responsibility
- Cooperation | Umoja - Unity
- Concern for Community - Imani - Faith

Speaking of cooperation, let's define that and analyze capitalism, yes? Per The Democracy Collaborative, the seven core principles of cooperatives are as follows:
- Voluntary/open membership
- Democratic control (1 member = 1 vote)
- Member economic participation
- Autonomy and independence
- Education, training and information
- Cooperation among cooperatives
- Concern for community

As you can see for yourself, the African principles line up perfectly with the seven core principles of cooperatives. This is a perfect example of what I spoke about in the "Returning to Our Roots" chapter - what we are reaching for now in attempts to decolonize our lives is not actually new at all. If no one else will say, I will - what we were doing before (colonization) was working. From what I can tell, there was rhyme and reason for the focused attention on cooperation as a pathway to build community. So, it's no wonder those principles are re-emerging now. Colonization, "power over", white supremacy culture, etc all benefits from a system in which some have and some do not have; a system in which there is a perception of competition so that an idea of lack will increase productivity + drive; a system in which privilege is based on skewing the results towards the ones in power to make up the rules. As I flash back to childhood memories over board games, it simply seems illogical and unethical to rig the game in your favor. But that's exactly what colonization is and does. As an entrepreneur with citizenship privilege in the USA, I do see the good in an enterprise- driven economy which is a core tenet of capitalism. However, when unearned power is not checked or distributed amongst the people most impacted, the system becomes more important than the people it was meant to serve in the first place. And this is where we find ourselves now. I suggest we take a post-capitalist approach and use our creativity to design something BEYOND what we have been accustomed to. Society and technology may have advanced, but we are leaving the institutions, systems and people behind. As we build anew, let us remember that abundance is our birthright and not something reserved for a select few.

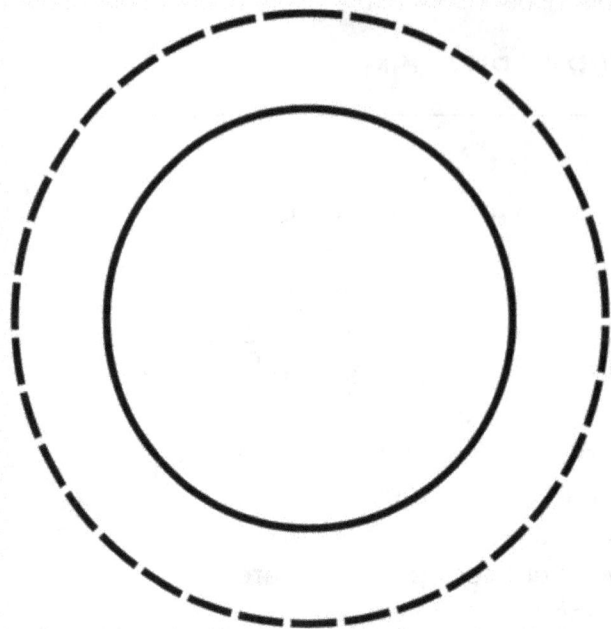

BUILD GENERATIONAL WEALTH

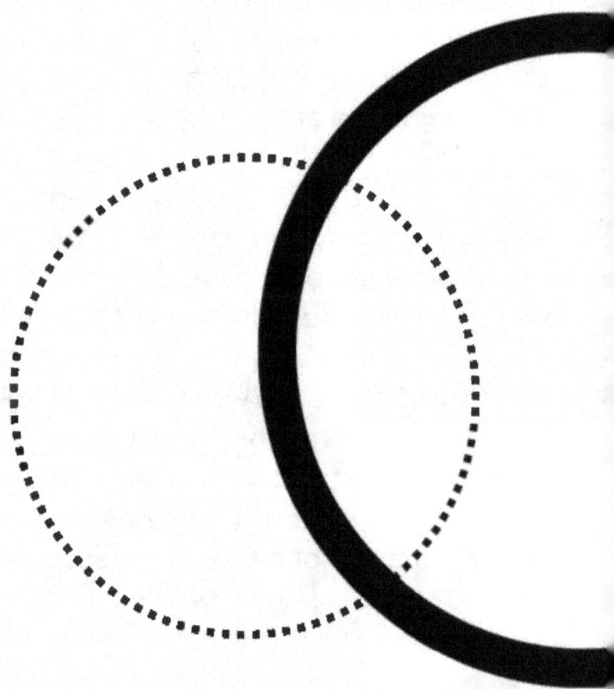

YOUR FIRST INVESTMENT: PAYING ATTENTION

Growing up, investments were not a common language at the dinner table, over holidays or a family gatherings. When I went off to college and evolved into adulthood, I started to be exposed to more folks talking about finances, financial advisement, investors, stocks + bonds, IRAs, 401Ks and retirement. It used to make my head spin. Nowadays, thankfully, there is more common language and resource sharing happening around building generational wealth that I think over the few decades, we will reach new levels of wealth by more people than we've ever seen before. However painful, my lack of awareness brought to my attention how few of us grew up with financial education. It wasn't taught in primary, middle or high school, unless you had a chapter of Junior Achievement, and not in college unless you were a Finance major. I have made many bad decisions when it comes to money, but as I fumble forward I commit to teach what I know to my siblings, my community and find ways to teach it to the little humans so they have a head start much sooner. Today, in addition to all the other things I'm up to (doing the MOST), I got a world-class financial education by studying for my life insurance broker exam. It woke me up in a way. I'm glad.

My late father, who had no life insurance, nothing saved and had only just been barely surviving on the money he had, taught me one of the greatest lessons of my life. He was buried only through the generosity and donations of churches, relatives and friends. That's right - we had to raise the money to bury my father. On top of the other aspects of grief I was already facing (be sure to chapter on "Grief is the Cost of Knowing Love" for how I got through that time), that added a whole other layer...and it woke up something that had been dormant inside of me. This is around the first time that I realized the first great act in investing wasn't stocks or bonds. It was about paying attention. What had he been paying attention to? What keeps us so occupied that we do not take the time to make proper arrangements for our death? Why is having car insurance more common than having life insurance? What do we miss out on in our lives simply because we weren't paying attention? There is much more I could say about all I have learned through my life insurance licensing process and the continuing education, but what is more important is for me to ring the bell for your wake up call. There will come a day when you are physically no longer here. Like change, death is a guarantee for all of us. What legacy will you leave behind for your family? The planet? How are you working toward that this very moment? As uncomfortable as it may be to face our mortality, the sooner we do the better we can prepare those who will carry on the family name, our work or our vision after us. First, we must call back our energy from distractions and make the best investment of our lives. I am so grateful to my father for this lesson I'll never forget. Pay attention.

TIME IS TRUE WEALTH

As you're reflecting on where your attention has been invested, I want to invite you to do a simple exercise. You may have seen a similar version before but engage as this will set up the work in the "Personal Niche Analysis" chapter a little later on . On the next page, I have left some open space for you to draw this out which you may choose to do, or use it as note taking space. You choose!

Start with a large circle (pie). Here are the instructions:
- Using the categories below, divide your pie into slices based on the amount of time you spend in a **week** on that area, totaling 168 hrs in a week (24 hrs x 7 days). *As an example, if you spend 40 hrs working, about 1/4 of your time pie will be labeled "Financial Capital".*
- **Social Capital** - deeds in relationships, family, friends
- **Material Capital** - home care, buildings, property
- **Financial Capital** - earning money, investing, working
- **Living Capital** - land work, animals/pets, nature
- **Intellectual Capital** - education, training, learning
- **Human Capital** - community, networking, group/club
- **Spiritual Capital** - worship, devotion, meditation, etc
- **Cultural Capital** - celebrations, holidays, gatherings

Use the space below for your pie drawing or note taking:

Before we turn the page on the chapter, take a moment to reflect on how this exercise felt as you were doing it. One thing I wanted to do for you was plant a seed that wealth is not just about money as there are at least eight forms of capital we all have access to (as adopted from *Appleseed Permaculture*). The other major takeaway here is to recognize that the wealthy are not just people with alot of money. The wealthy make their money work for them, instead of working for money in order to have **time freedom** to build wealth in other areas + enjoy life.

THE COST OF STAYING COMFORTABLE

Being comfortable seems dangerous to me and I have often had folks in my circle describe me as the kind of person that doesn't sit still for long...meaning that I'm always looking for the lesson, pursuing growth, aiming to be better than I was yesterday. I hate wasting time. I fully recognize that in order for us to find balance in life, we cannot always be in forward motion. Sometimes, it's going to require us to assume the Feminine position and reflect, post up where we are and wait for the action to find us. In our more masculine society, not doing or acting is HARD. When we get cozy in things staying as is, we quite literally go against nature which is always in perpetual motion. Just look at the seasons or the life cycle of seed. No two moments are the same. So take that metaphor and run with it like your life counts on it. Because it does. Life is out there, waiting for you to meet it halfway and ready to evolve you to your next level. Trust that if all of nature can surrender and push ahead, so too, can we. If change is something you struggle with, I invite you to take inventory of the price you're paying for keeping things as is. And then make a list of all that could be possible if you allow yourself to grow, in motion.

THE JOURNEY BACK
TO YOUR WORTH

Have you ever felt like the scum of the Earth? Even if just for a moment? Or like no one really "got" you so you had to bend and morph to be accepted? Or felt paralyzed by the possibility of rejection if you showed the real you? Assuming (which I prefer to rarely do) that your intent is pure and you mean no harm to yourself or others, who would you be hurting by existing and taking up space? Or maybe a better question is who would you be hurting by not taking up more space and being seen? Yourself, for certain. And possibly people who would benefit from the light and unique flavor you would bring into the world. And as we've been already touching on, the planet needs all hands on deck to lift this load we've acquired. So, if you felt like you needed someone to give you permission to be your quirky, weird, creative, free self consider this your hall pass. To you, from you. I know what it feels like to battle abandonment issues, anxiety around rejection and wounds from when you WERE yourself. Let me tell you a secret I recently discovered - you were ridiculed because you are special, unique, gifted and talented. Do not hide yourself away because you're not like anyone else. Authentic is the new normal.

Call on Mother Earth if you need to. All her children look different, but we cannot deny that there is an extreme precision and purpose our being right here. We must learn how to coexist amongst difference and appreciate the resources we have access to, daily. There is something here for you to do. Consider yourself the person to get it done. If you ever need a pick me up, bookmark this page:

I value me. I trust my inner voice. I give up the need to know. I am the source of my safety. I am the source of my own power. I am the source of my own money. I am the source of my own time. I am the source of my own spaciousness. I am the sources of my own wellbeing, health, wealth and everything good. I do not look to my partners, or my parents, or our government, or anyone else to be the source and cause agent for anything. I bring the power back to me because if I am relying on someone else to do that, I am at the whim and mercy of these people. It is my responsibility to keep myself happy and to meet my needs. I see my self-esteem as something for me to protect. I cultivate, value and protect my self-esteem. I value myself. I do not attach my self-esteem to any conditions because it is a sacred treasure. I take action, and I expose myself to things I am afraid of, and conquer it, and I take actions that protect my self-esteem in service to my highest well-being and self-care. Wherever I go, I bring my treasure with me....and I look outside of myself for nothing. I am connected to the Source. I am the source. And so it is.

Jade Rajbir Kaur

[Calling Back Your Worth | The Radiant Lotus]

DIVINE ALIGNMENT

Divine alignment for the Earth assignment is the tagline for House of SOLEIL. Divinity is not religious. Divinity is love, beauty and purpose. Do you cringe when I refer to you as Divine? During an interview with a beloved friend and colleague recently, I spoke on my initial resistance to being a "leader" because I had seen the chaos of popularity and was NOT interested, PLUS the thing that introverts want the most is to be cuddled up somewhere with a book, a journal, art and minding they business. Although I still err on the side of minding my business (or businesses to be technical!), I was graced by others' wisdom in my life and felt called by others to now share my wisdom. I believe each us of IS called to one thing or another and it is up to us to find out what gifts, treasure or wisdom are Divinely coded into us. The greatest gifts are often on the other side of the deepest wounds. Like some cruel, beautiful joke - the thing we run from most is usually tied to the thing we can most help others evolve through. To accept this new level of my journey, I had to completely surrender to the process and clear my life of people, places and things that were no longer aligned. Not everybody can come with us on the way up and if we're honest - would you want them to? If so, why? Guilt, codependency or familiarity? It's hard work to let things, people or relationships go that feel safe.

Once you are aligned, or as you're getting there, do not be mistaken that things will not be challenge. Your new life is going to cost you your old one. Think back to the divine balance and order I spoke about in "The 42 Divine Principles of Ma'at" chapter, yes? If you are expecting good things in life and your present situation does not reflect that, how will you get there? You will be asked to turn everything around you into rocket fuel to catapult you to where you want to go. If you clear space and still have expectations of life to make a special delivery, I can bare witness to the fact that your life will be cleared for you. I do not fully know how or why this works, but I've seen it enough times to call it truth. This may be why some people quote "faith without works is dead" - to request to receive without giving is not balanced. For me, the life, the peace, the joy and the creative freedom I have now cost me EVERYTHING. It was uncomfortable to have to compost friendships, relatives, my home + sanctuary, the comfort of old clients, old narratives, etc but if I'm truly a little baby seedling planted in/on Earth to grow to my greatest potential, how could I grow while planted in toxic soil? And no shade to the people I knew before, but the environment eventually had to evolve to match *my growth*. That's it. I let go, over and over again because I was determined to get aligned. Life is an adventure and I want to live mine out, fully. I'm still evolving in the direction I want to go, yet every day it gets a little easier. I want my life to be the result of courage, not comfort. Period. I choose to be myself because nobody else will give me permission to be. I count my blessings and witness all evidence of abundance in my life. So make your request, align your aim, compost your life into fuel and aim for the moon, beloved. You got this.

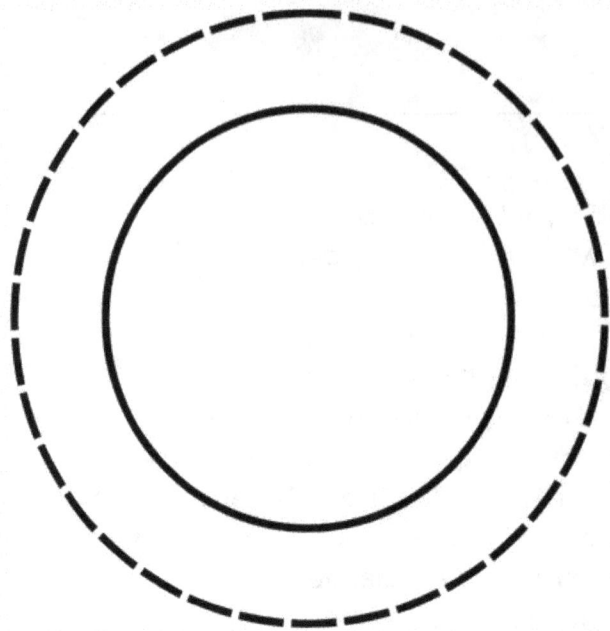

YOU HAVE A CHOICE

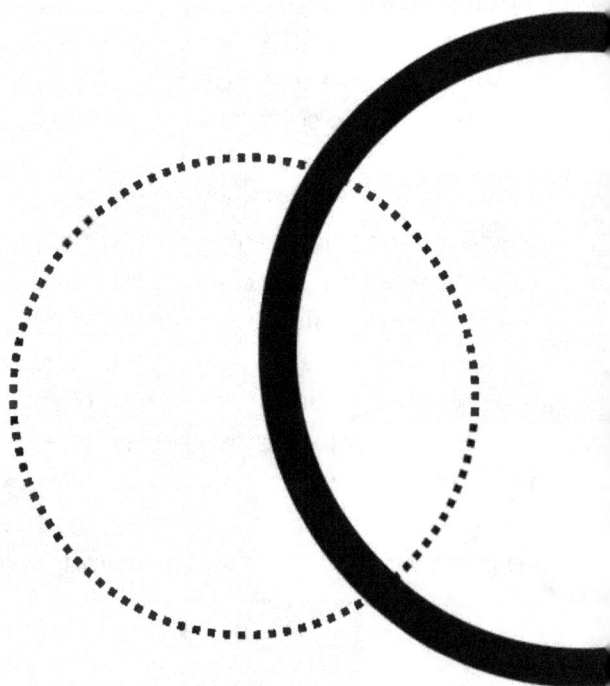

DESIGNING A PERSONAL NICHE [WEALTH] ANALYSIS

As we embark on this part of the journey, I first want to check that you did your homework? In other words, did you complete the exercise in the "Time is True Wealth" chapter? If not, pause here and go knock that out so that this flows more smoothly for you. You'll want your time pie chart handy as we start to dissect generational wealth. Now, as you will remember, we planted a major seed around this concept of what it means to be wealthy. Let me remind you - remove the words "poor", "broke", "underserved", "disadvantaged", "at-risk", "marginalized" and "lack" from your vocabulary RIGHT NOW. I love words and you way too much to continue allowing you to walk around speaking a reality that goes against your divine birthright, which is? That's right - abundant. The concept of lack, the idea of competition and the existence of poverty all have to do with the system structured around us called capitalism. Yet, capital itself takes on many other forms than money. Money, in fact, is financial capital and only one form of currency. Before we had money, exchanges happened with goods, seeds, livestock, crafts, skills and whatever else was of value. Reframing what wealth is brings that back to us a bit.

Some of you have probably heard it said that money is an energy and I have found this to be true. Money does not follow "safe" or comfortable. Money likes to FLOW like a river...it wants to be free and to land in clear containers. Money is an energetic state and it always responds to an energetic state. The more you make room for it with clear purposes for it to fulfill, the more it flows to you. So rather than hold onto a false belief that money is evil keep in mind that money responds to purpose. If you believe that money is bad and push it away from you energetically, will more or less of it show up for you? Instead recognize money as a collaborator in purpose. Some people don't do great things with money, but I deeply believe that more great people should have money. I for one, build businesses, re-distribute money to community and spend wisely so, money trusts me. I've been able to establish a new relationship as an adult in spite of my growing up in poverty and being in "lack".

All this said, pull out your time pie and look at the areas of your week (life) where you are investing most of your attention (and energy). What return or benefits is that bringing you? Are there any forms of capital where money COULD flow but you've denied it access? For example, if you have certain spiritual gifts that you've just been offering to people you love for free (Spiritual Capital section) and either don't feel comfortable asking for payment or never thought to, how can you invite money in as an energetic exchange? It cost YOU something to develop the skill you whether you paid for a training or simply invested the time into harnessing your craft.

Similarly to the times when goods and services were traded as forms of currency (or energetic exchange), you are bringing value to someone through your gift - saving them time, money or both - so you can and should be compensated for work and the upkeep of your craft. Is this starting to land for you? The other point I want to make as you're looking at your time pie is that any area that is visibly large (30% or more) is an area where you are investing a lot of time and attention, is essentially where you can trace your current wealth. You may be spiritually wealthy and financially poor. That's okay, because all it would take is the building of a container or structure for money to flow into to convert that investment of attention, time or energy into wealth. Which brings us back to the example of a spiritual gift suddenly becoming a spiritual business (i.e. coach, herbalist, yoga instructor, etc). Making sense? Ha!

I DO love a good pun. Now, if you have a large amount of time going into a specific type of capital but receiving little to no benefit, reciprocity or value that an areas that you might considering moving some of your investment somewhere else. Staying with the framing around attention and energy if, for example, you are investing alot of your time in the Financial Capital area (i.e. working long hours each week) but you don't have enough money or wealth to show for it that is a signal to see where else you can invest. Perhaps in Intellectual Capital by getting trained/educated on something you love or that has higher earning, perhaps in Social Capital to build up your network for referrals of clients or opportunities. These are all just examples, but you get the picture.

If you are partnered or share any responsibilities or Capital benefits with anyone, I would always suggest doing this analysis together with those people so that you all are on the same page, can keep one another accountable to any new plans you make and can develop a support system for when you meet bumps in the road.

The financial education and tools I'm offering you here are not to replace the advice of a wealth advisor, financial planner or investment firm if you already have these things in place. I will also add that my colleagues in the insurance industry, for the most part, share a similar creed that we simply want to help protect families, legacies, children and assets. Although I can technically call myself a financial professional and will continue to serve my clients + families in the way I wish someone would have sat down with my late father (more on that in "Your First Investment: Paying Attention"), this information is just the tip of the iceberg in reframing wealth. But, I would say it's a GREAT place to start, especially if you're not currently doing any financial planning...and most of the people you speak with in the finance world won't also be talking to you about ancestral healing, collective liberation and creative entrepreneurship all in one fell swoop. So, take my perspective, insights and wisdom with a grain of salt and remember to stay true to yourself by doing what resonates best for you. If you are on board to keep going and build on what I've shared so far, let's move on to breaking down the eight forms of capital as well as some permaculture design principles for your niche analysis.

First, let me back up and say that this concept of a Niche Analysis was first introduced to me from the world of permaculture design and because I understand Mother Nature as a teacher + all relations to be working together in an ecosystem, it was clear to me that this could be used to explain and inform wealth building for human-centered ecosystems as well. So what you're getting in this chapter is many years of study and refinement about how to lay this out in a way that would support me communicating to you abundance is always possible and all around, it all comes down to what we need, how we behave and therefore what we yield. Let me explain:

- A niche analysis is used to understand the many aspects and connections of a single element has within a larger system; a "niche" in the ecological sense of the word is "a position/role taken by a kind of organism within its community"; a "niche" in the business world/society is understood as your "lane"
- Your yield is that which you produce which can be physical but can also be less tangible like love or joy
- Your behaviors are those things you engage in to produce yields; or your actions out in the world or as part of the ecosystem that are meaningful.
- Your needs are what are necessary for happiness, a sense of belonging or connection; what creates stability and function; these can be physical, emotional or spiritual not just material.

All in all, by us doing a personal niche analysis around wealth-building, you are identifying the areas in the garden (ecosystem) of your life where you yield your needs and where there is little yields, behavior will shift.

Now, let's move on to the eight forms of capital. In the next few pages, I will lay out the types, an overview for each and some space for you to make your own notes. As with all content in my book, do check out the source list for more on concepts shared in this chapter. Here we go:

1 SOCIAL CAPITAL

Influence, connections and the accessibility to 'favors', decision-making or relationship building.

2 MATERIAL CAPITAL

Non-living physical objects including natural resources, buildings, bridges and technology.

3 FINANCIAL CAPITAL

Money, securities, credit cards, bank accounts, investments, stocks, bonds or access to funds.

4 LIVING CAPITAL

Animals, plants, water and soil of our land; the basis for life on the planet and your stewardship

5 INTELLECTUAL CAPITAL

Knowledge, education, learning, training, science, research, preparation for your life or life's work

6 EXPERIENTIAL CAPITAL

Organizing projects or service with community, collaboration, cooperation or mutual aid

7 SPIRITUAL CAPITAL

Spiritual or religious practices, connection to Self, the universe, divinity, praise, worship, devotion

8 CULTURAL CAPITAL

Traditions, gatherings, holidays, celebrations, rites of passage, other milestone markers of a people

THE FOUR ARCHETYPES
OF AUTHORITY

Congratulations on making it to this part of the journey! In the previous chapter we were talking a lot about energy, attention, investment, sowing seeds, ecosystems, producing and wealth so naturally, the next place to go is up. Whether you are self-made, an entrepreneur, or an authority in your own life some other way, I want to make sure you can articulate that authority and sustain the empire we've been working so hard to build. As you prepare to be the CEO of your life, repeat after me:

I take my place. I create space for me. I sit upon my throne, and integrate my lover, warrior, magician + sovereign to guide me forward. I know that the Earth and all the elemental forces are behind me as well. I hold all the power. I hold all the cards, and the codes are all within me, and I HAVE A MASTERPIECE TO CREATE. I can do this NOW. I vow to honor my commitments. I vow to honor my boundaries. I vow to honor my peace, no matter what it takes to protect. I vow to value and protect my treasure, my genius and my gifts. I vow to value my creativity and my home. I am ready NOW.

[ ] LOVER DOMAIN: DREAM.

Overseer of wealth. Here creativity begets legacy.

POWER STATEMENT: I am lover. I am rooted in love, desire, values, worth and sacrifice. My opinions, thoughts and beliefs are not for sale. I value me.

Where in your life or work do you show up as CFO, or money handler? Any shifts you would like to make?

[ ] WARRIOR DOMAIN: WIELD.

Overseer of space. Here freedom flows in choice.

POWER STATEMENT. I am warrior. I am rooted in boundaries, will, support, limits, resources + space. I will do what I must, no matter what it takes.

Where in your life or work do you show up as HR, or resource builder? Any shifts you would like to make?

[ ] MAGICIAN DOMAIN: WEAVE.

Overseer of speech. Here lies authentic, soul truth.

POWER STATEMENT: I am magician. I am rooted in reality, knowing, time, creativity, alchemy, intuition + creativity. I know what I know. I am certain.

Where in your life or work do you show up as PR, or network builder? Any shifts you would like to make?

[ ] SOVEREIGN DOMAIN: DECREE.

Overseer of time. Here lies balanced, fruitful rhythm.

POWER STATEMENT: I am sovereign. I am rooted in vision, identity, decrees and dreams. I am my power source, no one else. I honor who I am.

Where in your life or work do you show up as CEO, leader, visionary? Any shifts you would like to make?

LEGACY BUILDING

We are well on our way to relieving the burden from the backs of your future children, grandchildren and the youth of today. Thank you for the work you are putting, or will put, into doing your part to clean up our mess. It's never too late and never too early if you ask me. But this isn't just about me! It's about the beautiful strides we will make *together*, as a collective with a shared mission and vision. In the journey on the pages of this book, we've been laying a solid foundation, brick by brick so no wolf can come along and blow your house down. I mentioned legacy building in several chapters with other framing. Here, I want to make space to make sure that you have things you can begin to act on and look into so that all the hard work you've been up to can truly become a playbook or strategic plan for the future. I know all too well how many of us are NOT having these conversations in our families and unfortunately, that only burdens those we leave behind. Take a lesson from my father. So, allow me to plant a seed so that you have a starting point for your garden of alignment and abundance. Together, we can make things better for ALL OF US. And also, sleep better at night knowing that your family, assets and impact will continue contributing to the planet after you.

If you already have a family financial advisor or someone who is reviewing your insurance policies, assets, investments or savings plan, take this list to them to review together (or with your notes) and add to this as needed:

BUILDING, PROTECTING + PRESERVING YOUR LEGACY:

- Do you have a life insurance policy? If so, do you know the benefits, which type and if it has a cash value?

- If you are a CEO or own a business, do you have Key Person Insurance policy on yourself?

- Are your children, spouse, home or debts insured?

- Have you written out a Will & Testament?

- Have you selected and named a Power of Attorney?

- If you own a business, do you have an EIN #; Certificate of Assumed Name; legal status; Duns & Bradstreet #; professional email; phone (not a cell); non-resident mailing address; 411 listing; and registered with NAV? You'll need it all for credibility.

- Have you taken steps to protect your ideas + property?

- Do you have all of your important documents compiled and easy to grab in case of fire or flood?

- Does your family have emergency plan/phone tree?

- If you can no longer make decisions, who is next in line?

RELATIONSHIP BUILDING

If the "Legacy Building" chapter did not make it clear, relationships are EVERYTHING and no one person can do it all alone. After all this time that you've spent with me, I would happily invite you to consider me as someone in community with you now. There are many ways for us to continue building our relationship beyond the pages of this book, but as a sovereign, autonomous being it will be up to you to further extend that invitation for connection. You can find me nestled up real cozy over at House of SOLEIL ade PROJECT, Cortina Jenelle Branding Agency, OSHANNA, on the podcast, YouTube channel, Wisdom, LinkedIN, Moonchild Nature School, the SOL community and of course just a old school email or phone call. There are many, many ways to engage, just pick what resonates with you and I'll meet you halfway. Beyond me, there are others like you who have picked up this book and are compelled to take action. I would be happy to be a conduit in making any connections that might be helpful. Don't forget to build out your support map as you take action on the work we've done here. Turn the page for a few tips on relationship building and networking that have served me well over the years. It's not time to say goodbye just yet, by any means. Happy relating, beloved!

NETWORKING FOR AUTHENTIC RELATIONSHIPS:

- **Be yourself!** This may seem like common sense but sometimes it's easier to "fake it to you make it". I do not suggest faking anything as with all attraction, you will only get more "fake it to you make it" around you.
- **Do things your inner child loves.** You never know who you will meet when you allow your curiosity to lead.
- **Seek out communities around skills you hope to acquire or learning.** (i.e. Toastmasters, SkillShare, Teachable, etc). Like minded people already there!
- **Seek out events or gatherings where you can add value** (i.e. Eventbrite, Meetup, LinkedIN Groups, etc). Take the brave step and introduce yourself to the organizers. Sometimes volunteering leads to more!
- **Give back in a way that pays forward the hands that helped you** (i.e. speaking at AA meetings after you've gotten sober; taking shifts for crisis lines that you once had to call yourself; donate gently used clothes to Goodwill, etc) Not only will it feel good for your heart and spirit to serve, you may build bonds that give you the confidence to show up MORE in life.
- **Start a community** (if that's your thing). Great platforms like Mighty Networks, Discord, YouTube, Wix and other sites make it fun to host members.
- **Other ideas that you want to try out:**

ENTREPRENEURSHIP AS LIBERATION

My goodness, beloved. I can hardly believe that we have arrived at the last official chapter of the book. It has been quite the journey and I hope that as we move into our conversation about entrepreneurship as liberation that you feel full of possibilities, ideas, support, strength, wisdom, your unique genius and a bounty of resources. Beyond this chapter, there is a "Toolkits" section that provide you with some how-tos, guides, checklists and strategies that can be incorporated into your life to make more space for the new and to support this evolution. And beyond that beyond is a "What Now?" section where you can find my Acknowledgements, About the Author, more Bonus Offers + Client Testimonials. The work does not stop here, my friend. This is just the beginning.

Liberation enters our lives in a slow drip, not a waterfall. If you look and listen carefully enough, you can see the areas where the internal + external work you have been doing to unlearn harmful programming and unhealthy practices has already begun to loosen its grip on you. The rest of the way to liberation is solely up to you. It will require moving in the dark. The light will return always.

When I was 12 years old, I had no idea that there was a seed being planted deep down on the inside of me. I thought I was just picking up a summer job working for my grandmother's catering business. So much about it I loved. I got to travel with her to festivals, events, gatherings of many kinds. I got to work (my Capricorn moon LOVES to work). I got to earn money. More importantly, I was learning the ins and outs of running a business, community organizing and how to serve people with excellence. There was no slack given. Even though I was the youngest on the team, I was determined to earn my keep so I worked hard and watched. And listened. And observed. Fast forward 15 yrs later, I was finishing grad school with a Masters of Arts in Business Management + Leadership and simultaneously starting my first business. That same year, I won the Emerging Entrepreneur of the Year award and was inducted into 40 Under Forty for my around business, community, leadership and economics. I was 27 years old. My grandmother was 54 years old when she started her catering business. She was the first and only Black women from our rural mountain town I knew that had her own business and it was wildly popular. Although the business had a short run, the seed had been planted in me and by her bringing me along on her journey, I picked up the assignment in half the time it took her. In November 2019, I invited my grandmother up to one of my events. We were having the celebration for the Celebrating African-Americans through Public Art and it was in The Block (neighborhood) at Eagle-Market Street in Asheville, NC. On that very same block, 20 years earlier,

I had stood beside her in our tent at Goombay Festival, serving our hungry and happy customers just as fast as she could cook. That very SAME BLOCK. It was surreal. We both felt the parallel timeline shift that night and at one point while she was socializing and having a good time in the full room of supporters, my team members and artists while I was on the mic, we exchanged a smile. At the end of the night when it was all done, she said to me "Wow, this was really something", and to her I smiled and said "I wanted you to see that I listened and you taught me well". I'll never forget that moment and I will forever remain humble for it. My grandmother made many sacrifices in her lifetime in order to raise her 6 children, co-parent grandchildren (me included), keep up with friends, neighbors, church responsibilities, a house, a garden, chores and all the family holidays. She did it all. As best she could. One thing I also never forgot was that she loved to write. Never did have the chance to pursue or publish her writing because duty called, but in her pursuing entrepreneurship she liberated me and as I showed her the harvest on the inside of me, I know I liberated her, too. May her legacy live on in bounty.

On a final word, it goes with saying that I know and feel deep in my bones that entrepreneurship is liberation. Not only does it create time freedom, break cycles of "poverty", it creates new worlds of possibility and a place where dreams can grow wings to become REALITY. There are countless stories of folks that went from rags to riches and guess what? They are ALL entrepreneurs. So if you've ever wanted to a leap, no time like the present! YOU can heal the planet from wherever you are, beloved.

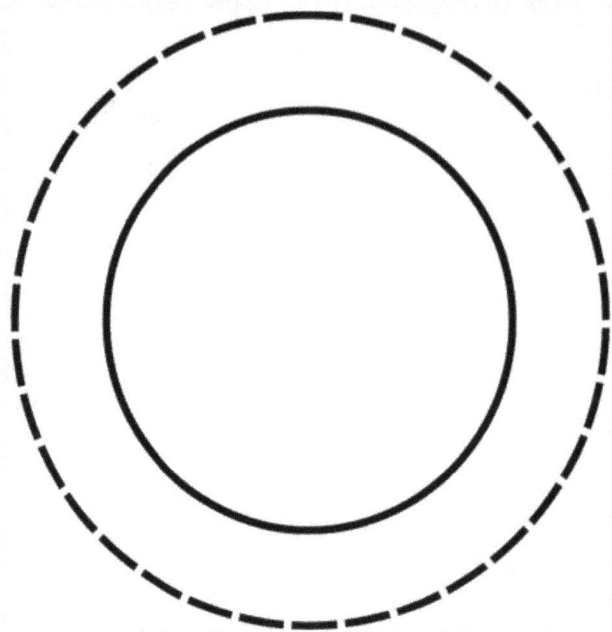

TOOLKITS

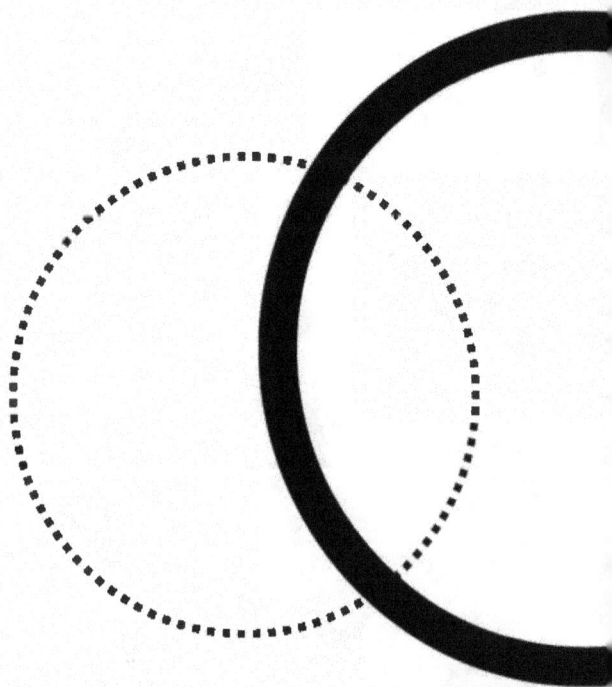

Human-Centered Work Lives

These days, many of us are relying on virtual technology, virtual assistants, virtual calls and other resources that challenge our traditional work styles in order to show up for our work in an increasingly globally connected world. Rather than dive right into the agenda, reports, numbers, performance and productivity, take into consideration ways you can humanize + decolonize your meetings. This way, people truly feel seen, heard, valued for who they are, not simply just what they can do for you. Using tools from Creative Facilitation, as passed down by PYE Global, YES! World and teaching artistry, here are starter ideas:

- Establish clear agreements about holding space.
- At the start of meetings, reserve the first 10 minutes for a check-in or grounding exercise. Rotate out fun or creative check-in questions that build trust and relationships amongst the team; or do breathwork.
- Establish ways to bring the group back to attention or get attention for the group to get quiet. Adopt them.
- For in-person meetings, arrange the space in a circle instead of a linear setting with a "head of table".
- Include reflection time in meetings by posing questions and doing timed free-writing; offer longer bio breaks; or don't request decisions be made on the spot - this will be more inclusive for introverted processors or those who need more time to chime in.

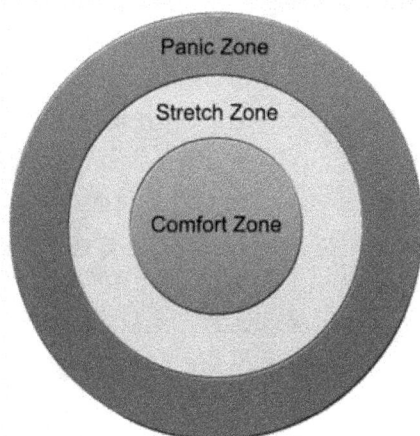

The **comfort zone** is the zone in which an individual feels comfortable. There is no fear or discomfort. The person feels at home, comfortable and safe. All things are familiar. Within this zone there are no challenges to start a learning process. Things stay the same, unquestioned.

The **stretch zone** is the zone in between the previous zones. In this zone things (activities, situations,...) feel somehow awkward and unfamiliar. In this zone learning can occur. It is the zone where you can enhance your possibilities + where you can explore your boundaries.

In the **panic zone** a challenge is so far away from the zone in which we feel comfortable, that it becomes overwhelming. In this zone we experience stress, fear and challenge in a way that learning is impossible (for instance our fight or flight reaction). All our energy is spent on managing and controlling our fear and panic. When someone is here, there is a trigger or wound.

For moments when the feelings feel like too much:

I call upon the unconditionally loving guidance that can assist me, with mercy, grace, protection and support, through my ascension process. I accept this opportunity to grow spiritually and shift from one reality to a higher vibrational reality. I accept the opening of my chakras into a more loving consciousness. I accept the changes happening in me and in my life to aid in this spiritual growth. May I be held in tenderness and compassion as I release lower vibrational patterning and embody my authentic divinity. May the beings of unconditional love that ground the loving rainbow be invited to do so now. Through my free will, so be it. And so it is.

- Identify the feeling or thought.
- Identify the trigger connected to the feeling or thought.
- Identify which action I can take from my divine intervention list.
- Identify three people I trust and feel comfortable calling in from my support map.
- Identify professional people/resources that I can call on for additional support.
- Make a gratitude list of what I will be grateful for as I continue to feel, reveal and heal.

Have you ever had a moment that jolted you into flight or fight mode and you were quickly looking for a way to bring you back to center? I call this a divine intervention. So that life doesn't keep knocking you off your square, make a list and keep it handy so you can ground. Here are some ideas to jumpstart your divine intervention list:

- Take a bath or a long shower.
- Put on calming music.
- Go for a walk in nature.
- Take a nap.
- Make some art.
- Play or take your inner child on a play date.
- Drink some water.
- Write down all the negative self talk or critique running through your mind. Then go back over the words on the page to reframe them as positive.
- Go for a run or sign yourself up for a fitness class.
- Put on your favorite song and dance to it.

OTHER NOTES OR IDEAS THAT WORK FOR YOU:

How to Setup Open Space Technology

TIME - 1+ hours (or as long as you wish)

GROUP SIZE – 15+ // MATERIALS - Notecards or post-its, large poster paper, pens/markers, tape

WHY?
At any given point in your gathering, your participants will have a sense of the conversations they want to have or activities they want to do. Open Space Technology (OST) is a way to help your group self-organize into participant-instigated and participant-led discussions, workshops or explorations. It lets people make their private conversations public, by letting the whole group know what they are interested in and inviting others to join them. Its simple and elegant principles create a wide space within which to engage. OST is often a highlight of a gathering, as it supports self-designed learning at all levels.

HOW?
The best part of a conference was the coffee breaks. That was where people had a chance to meet and explore the topics they were most interested in. We get to self-organize now and make public the conversations + activities we want right now!

Now, pass out a notecard or post-it to each person, along with a pen or marker. "You are going to write down, in short, what you want to do. It can be something you want to learn or share/teach. You don't need to be an expert to host a session. You can have a question, activity or it can just be something you want to explore further. You are only committing to opening the space; ultimately, what happens will be co-created by the people who come to your space... Take a few minutes to give it thought. Then, write that down on your post-it."

Give the group a few minutes to reflect and write.

Then, the facilitator starts up again: "Now, I am going to invite people to trust me, as I guide you through the set-up. It might feel a little hairy or strange at moments, but I want you to know that it will work out. Just give it a few minutes, and we'll be all set."

Based on the time you have, you will need to determine whether you will have one, two or more slots of time. Typically, you want 45-60 minutes per slot; so, for example, if you have a two-hour time frame, you'll have two 50-minute slots to work with, after the set-up, which takes about 20 minutes. If you have less time, or more time, you can adjust your time slots. Just be sure to have equal amounts of time allotted for each slot.

Ask whoever feels ready to start. They will stand up and take 15-20 seconds to name their activity/discussion topic. You will ask them where they want to do this, and they will name a location on your site. (You can have 4-5 locations in mind to help out, if needed.) You ask them which time slot they want to do this in, if there is more than one time slot. You then place/tape their card on the large paper, which indicates the time slot and location. Then, another person is invited to go. And, so on. Depending on the size of your group, you can decide how many offerings you will have per time slot. Typically, in a group of 30, you will have 5-6 offerings per time slot.

Usually, after the third or fourth person has shared, then a few members of the group may begin to freak out -- usually because they want to go to more than one offering. You can gently but firmly remind them of the Law of Two Feet and the other principles, and reassure them that it will all work out. Also, usually after 5-6 offerings have been made, most of the group is satisfied because they know of at least one offering they want. Once you have 5-6 offerings per time slot, go through and review them one more time, in short, and then release the group to Open Space. Let the fun begin!

If you have a second time slot, let them know five minutes prior to and at the start of that time slot, to go ahead and switch and start the next set of offerings.

Four Principles + The Law of Two Feet

1.Whoever comes are the right people. This means, appreciate whoever is there, and don't worry about who is not. Whoever is there with you in the moment is exactly who should be.

2.Whatever happens is the only thing that could have. Too often, we miss it because we are governed by expectations. This principle frees us up. We don't need to worry about what could have been; we get to rest in what is /was and be there.

3.When it starts, it starts. Whenever it is is the right time.

4.When it's over, it's over. No need to stretch it out. If you feel complete in 10 minutes, you're done. If you need more time, you can create more time. Be alive to what's truly there, not beholden to time.

There is also one law in **OST: The Law of Two Feet.** This means that you use your two feet to go wherever you can learn and contribute the most. You can move around to different groups, stay with one the whole time, or join none of them. Bottom line: You are 100% responsible for your experience.

It's good to write the four principles and The Law of Two Feet onto a piece of paper for everyone to see and reference -- especially because they are not just crucial for OST, but are also wonderful principles to remember and apply in everyday life. Learn more about Open Space Technology at openspaceworld.org.

Gratitude is a POWERFUL magnet for attracting more of what you want in your life by putting your attention on that which you already have, and APPRECIATE. Here are some ways to practice gratitude in your life:

- Make a gratitude list of 5 things you are grateful for today - either do it as you wake or before bed at night.
- Create a gratitude collage in place of, or addition to, your vision boarding at the end of the year with images of all that you've been grateful for.
- Say thank you. When someone holds the door open for you. When someone hands you your change. When you want to pray but have no words. When something unexpected shows up. Say thank you.
- Send someone a handwritten postcard, letter or thank you card, appreciating them.
- Create a gratitude bank out of an old shoebox or jar. Add decor! Everytime something happens you're grateful for happens, write it down and drop it in.

And on a last note - gratitude will not always be easy to come by. If you do this enough or at least start, you can review your lists, collages or gratitude banks on the hard days which for me, always sparked MORE gratitude!

Kemetic yoga refers to the entire spiritual system of self-development created by the sages of ancient Egypt. It is a worldview that recognizes the nature of reality and our place in the universe. Kemetic Yoga is the understanding of our connection to the spirits of our ancestors and the 5 true nature of Divine Universal Forces (Deities properly called Neteru). From this perspective we recognize that there is an omnipotent and unknowable creative mind called Neter from which all in the universe comes from.

Religious minds attempt to call this unknowable Mind a being (named God) and give it a human personality. Our ancestors in ancient Kemet simply accepted that this force is beyond our human ability to fully grasp and were content with this acknowledgement of human limitation. At the same time they recognized that this universal force manifested itself in a myriad of ways.

These manifestations of Neter (where we get the word nature) are the forces of nature. These are galaxies, constellations, stars, planets and the elements of Earth, Air, Fire and Water. They are those ascended spiritual beings that lived in physical form thousands or even millions of years ago in epochs when the possibility of human potential was much greater and they were able to reach tremendous heights of spiritual consciousness and power far beyond our current ability to comprehend.

The word "yoga" literally means control. When we do not have control over our thoughts and behaviors, we become unhappy and out of balance. Lack of control over one's thoughts is related to the definition of insanity. Once we incorporate the philosophic principals of Kemetic Yoga™ into our daily lives, not only do we learn how to control our thoughts and relaxation techniques, but we train our bodies not to respond to stress or stressful situations. Kemetic Yoga™ teaches you the skill to ease yourself into a posture as opposed to forcing yourself into it. Most importantly, Kemetic Yoga™ emphasizes control of the breath.

....

"Changing consciousness is the pathway to changing behavior. Shift mind to shift heart. Once you realize your power, then you need to actualize by planning. The key objectives are an ethic of wellness...the keys are to distress, create a life of wellness, and the proper mindset to be resilient and breathe. You have to engage the body but first you have to retrain it in order for it to do so. The ultimate goal of yoga is to teach an ethic of wellness. True mastery is being able to cultivate a state of bliss long term...train the body to disengage from fight or flight. Reconnect to the breath. Remove ailing stimuli. Be in the world but not of it. To not be moved, or to not react to the shifts and changes happening around you...that is mastery. That is alignment, and that is the medicine that yoga + breathwork offer us."

Yirser Ra Hotep
Founder of Yoga Skills Method + Kemetic Yoga™

OTHER NOTES:

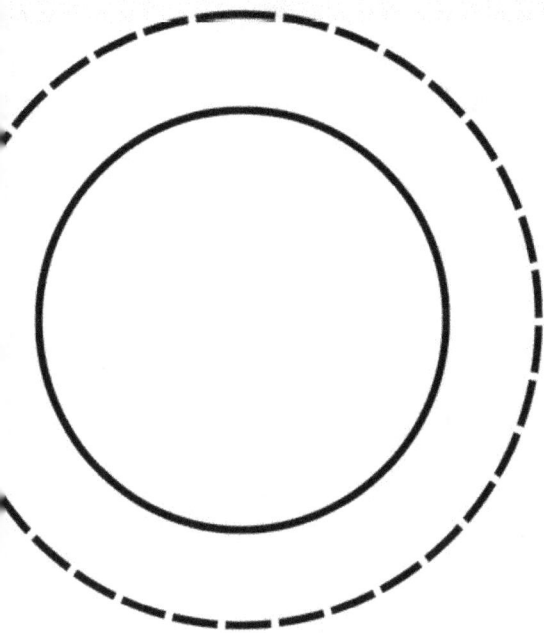

WHAT NOW?

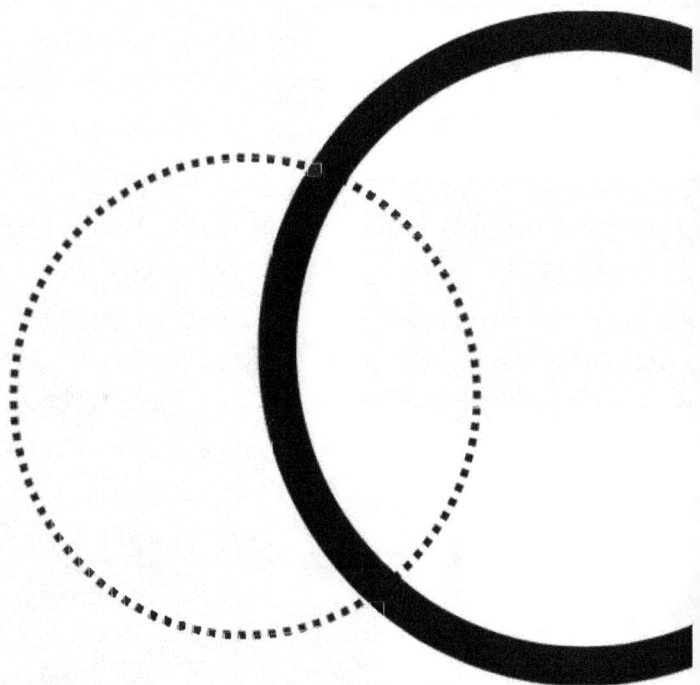

FREE MINI-JOURNAL
FOR REFLECTION + NOTETAKING

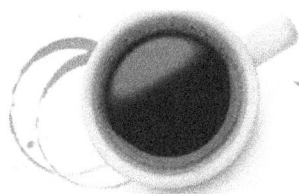

REFLECTION JOURNAL

CORTINA JENELLE CALDWELL

how to
HEAL
THE PLANET
from wherever you are

ANCESTRAL HEALING THROUGH BREATHWORK

Over 10 years ago, I was diagnosed with discoid lupus, polycystic ovarian syndrome, pre-diabetes and given a warning from doctors that my body was facing serious recourse, possibly an early death, if I did not change my habits and get my health in check immediately. After having my moment of despair, I made a plan to bring my health back into balance and set out on a life-changing journey to learn how to take care of myself. I had seen so many family members die young or face terminal illnesses so, I decided that ended with me. I didn't know how to take care of myself, but I was committed to learning. I felt I had to. In the span of less than 2 years, I lost about 100 pounds, picked up a yoga practice, moved to an ecovillage to learn to live from the land and started seeing holistic and healing arts practitioners. Today, I am in the best shape of my life, farm avidly, can apply holistic remedies with ease and often get mistaken for being 10+ years younger than I am! I have truly reclaimed my life.

Although this book shares strategies that will help you shape change, the turning over of physical health so that you can show up for your life needs a hands-on approach. For those who are ready for a life-changing experience, I offer private sessions, virtually or in-person, where we use yoga, breathwork and my facilitation skills to design a life of holistic wellness that you can sustain and share widely.

BRING SOCIAL PERMACULTURE TO YOUR COMMUNITY

About permaculture, Professor Stuart B. Hill of the University of Western Sydney NSW Australia states, "Instead of repeatedly wasting expertise, time, energy and resources in efforts to address such problems, at the 'back-end' of the system, permaculture enables us to avoid and minimize them by focusing on 'front-end' imaginative design and redesign initiatives." In other words, our creativity can shape our world and in fact, has. So, what will you create? Is your focus community need, social causes, your family, inner work, spreading joy? However you live out your most benevolent purpose, I can promise you that the world is better for you sharing it. In my own life, I wanted to design a life beyond the limitations of what other people told me was possible. As a result, I have traveled the world, built incredible relationships, supported some beautiful communities, discovered incredible natural resources. And yet, the best of these is the time I spend coaching servant leaders.

As a reader of this book, you have already primed the soil to root into the ethos deeper and go about *putting info into action*. Whether you want to design a strategic plan, business plan, community bylaws, mentor students or plan a conference, I am here to help make the aspects of permaculture, abundance, inclusion and growth real for you and your team. Let's build your sustainable future!

ACKNOWLEDGEMENTS

It truly does take a village. I have heard many people say that no one who succeeds at anything great does it alone. At no point in my life have I been without a helping hand, wisdom or love pouring into me. As someone raised in a village of elders, neighbors, teachers, clergy, friends and nature itself - I affirm that with my life. Because I believe in the old saying that "what goes around, comes around", I also have to believe that when we are up to good things from a positive place, the universe truly does conspire in our favor to support our dreams. I am grateful for the opportunity to become an author and to share my work and message more widely.

On the note of people, I truly have so many more to thank than I can list so for that, I ask for grace. I'm certain more names will come about in my next book(s) (hint hint!) so know that you are appreciated regardless, for the part you played in my growth and development. For starters, I want to thank the following authors, speakers and teachers who shaped my young mind and planted seeds of curiosity about the big questions in life. You made it possible for a little black Queer girl in the rural South to believe in something larger than life and then to go about roadmapping her way to success:

Sobonfu Somé, Marianne Williamson, Don Miguel Ruiz, Neale Donald Walsch, Octavia Butler, Dr. Maya Angelou, Langston Hughes, Resmaa Menakem, Jack Canfield, Martha Beck, Elizabeth Gilbert, Julia Cameron, Rev. Pat Bacon, Ann M. Martin, Iyanla Vanzant, Michelle C. Johnson, J.K. Rowling, Pema Chodron, Stephen R. Covey, David Holmgren, Brené Brown, Mitch Albom, Christine Guiterrez, Khalil Gibran and Rebecca Campbell.

I thank the following communities that welcomed me with open arms and showed me how beautiful humanity is as I traveled the world as spiritual SOL-journer: Earthaven Ecovillage; The Lava Sanctuary; B-Love's Guest House; La Casa Zapote; Bufo Alvarius Sanctuary; The Hostel in the Forest; 8th Life Panama; Highlander Center; Mountain Light Sanctuary; Art of Living Retreat Center; UR Light Center; Sweet Peas Hostel; Negril SOV Resort; Ahhh! Ras Nantango Garden + Gallery; Geddes Great House; Soweto Inspirational Home Museum and Anakato Hotel - our work and time together shaped this book.

And last but certainly not least, I want to thank my cadre of mentors and creative investors - Jennifer Pickering, for seeing my potential; Dorothy Randall Gray, for helping me heal my relationship with writing; Cat Shepard, for helping me to transmute my pain into art; Miranda Wildman, for inspiring me to marry my love of nature with my creativity; Nadia Payan, for sanctuary; to Nancy + Joseph Hasty, for being angels disguised as teachers and your unwavering belief in my greatness; and my clients and students over the years who believed. I'm grateful!

ABOUT THE AUTHOR

Words were my first love. Growing up you could find me either outside on imaginary adventures with the neighborhood kids or in my room immersed in a book, insatiable in my thirst for knowledge and understanding things beyond my experience. Bookworms were celebrated at my elementary school and I often took home first place prize for most books read over the summer breaks which then earned me a coupon for a personal pan pizza from Pizza Hut, a frostie from Wendy's or a happy meal from Burger King. Even though what I put into my body is quite different now, the seed planted in me from so long ago was showing me that being a bookworm came with rewards, has never left me. Even still, like most of us, I fumbled my way along with my calling with writing and sharing my story. When I was younger, the sacred space of my diary was violated and got me into trouble, simply for authoring my own truth, reflection and feelings. Over the past 25 years, I have been healing that wound and have slowly made a return to words and writing. This book is a homecoming for me.

If you are like me, you might have flipped to this section of the book first to learn a little bit more about the person you're about to spend alot of time with. I get it! For those reasons, I wanted this section of the book to both be written in my voice, addressing you - the shepherd of the life the book will take on beyond me - and share my more professional experiences that informed *How to Heal the Planet from Wherever You Are: Leaning into the Cosmic + Planetary Link Between Ancestral Healing, Collective Liberation + Creative Entrepreneurship* in the first place. I know us millennials have a bad stereotype for being noncommittal, lazy, apathetic and just overall unreliable but the truth is, values matter more to us millennials than blind loyalty. Many of us feel unwilling to participate in the/any abuse of power while ignoring the suffering it causes others. So while you may not see our capes, it is our challenge of inequitable status quo that will cement our legacy in the end. Our principles and values are not for sale and book is written with that ethos in mind. Our generation and those behind us have come to balance the world and perhaps take the risks that our parents, grandparents and ancestors could not. I honor them DEEPLY because it is on their shoulders I stand. I also say from my millennial mind and heart that we can do better. Not out of laziness, but because we DO care - about ourselves, about the planet and about the future we inherit every day. So the next time you connect with a millennial, as opposed to casting a judgement or stereotype , invite them into your decision-making circles and ask their perspective. I guarantee you it will be monumental for all. Diversity is a measure of our wealth.

WHAT MY CLIENTS + STUDENTS SAY

This gave me alot. It's the first [business] program of this kind I've ever been able to finish and definitely gives me a hopeful outlook about what's possible from here. Enjoyed it, it was smooth! Elements all worked together even though everyone was in a different place with their business. I really like how it was all put together. The greatest thing in life is knowing your purpose and following your cause & dreams. Thanks, Cortina!

Clarence Robinson
COOKING WITH COMEDY, FOUNDER

I am ready to fulfil this need in this food industry here. We are lacking and I am tired of doing without. It's time. I have been in business for 6 years as a caterer...it's time to advance. This has been an eye-opening experience. It forces me to step outside of my regular thinking pattern and pivoted my thoughts down a new alley of business ownership I never considered. Awesome job and program Ms. Cortina!!!!!

Romona Yong
KENTE KITCHEN + GROCERY, FOUNDER

Cortina brings fresh ideas, a unique way of looking at things and effective problem solving skills. She provides solutions to challenges faced by many...her grasp on matters of equity is extraordinary and follow-through is consistent. I have been amazed at what I have seen her create.

Cleaster Cotton
INTERNATIONALLY-ACCLAIMED ARTIST

Overall, I just want to say thank you for all of your support, and help, and guidance! This program and experience has been great. I came into it not knowing what to expect and I'm leaving it with new connections, inspiration and so much more.

Anna Zuevskaya
ASHEVILLE-BUNCOME COMMUNITY LAND TRUST, FOUNDING DIRECTOR

For me, this is legacy work. I learned so much invaluable information from this cohort. I made many amazing connections, and I brought others into this work as well. The most important thing about what I do is transforming lives, and assisting people in experiencing what it means to truly thrive in their lives. Thank you for the opportunity, the awesome playlist during sessions, and all that you did for each of us!

Marcus Kirkman
THE ROOT WELLNESS & COUNSELING, FOUNDER& LEAD PRACTITIOMER

Cortina has received recognition as a ICAgile Professional (2023) for work with human-centered design; inaugural cohort member of Periscope Chattanooga (2023-24); a CoThinkk Community Leader Award Nominee (2021); Tzedek Impact Award Winner (2020-2019); KNOW Global Women of the Year (2020); WNC Women Leadership Award in Art + Culture(2019); Leadership Asheville nominee (2014); 40 Under Forty: Asheville (2013); and WNC Minority Enterprise Development's Emerging Entrepreneur of the Year (2012). In addition to holding a Doctorate of Divinity, Masters in Management & Leadership, Cortina is a certified Kemetic Yoga Instructor, certified Creative Facilitator, licensed Insurance Producer & Financial Professional and rigorously trained in diversity, equity, inclusion. In addition, Cortina's work has been most noted for its undeniable creative skill, thoughtful intention on building community across difference and lasting impact on the spaces and people touched in the process. Her collective body of work has including grassroots cooperative building workshop for the National Guild on Community Arts Education; a feature role in community play Transitions; published poetry "Dear Black Church" and "Dear America"; a year in residence at Earthaven Ecovillage, an intentional community on 300 acres of sacred land in Western North Carolina; production of "Black Starseed" in collaboration with PechaKucha Asheville; community facilitator for the Vance Monument Task Force and public input process in Asheville, NC; earning Partners in Education status for a community arts-rooted educational program with the Kennedy Center; founding a nationally recognized Youth Leadership Program; serving with Black Lives of UU and so much more. For a full bio or professional CV, visit Cortina on the web or on LinkedIN.

www.ingramcontent.com/pod-product-compliance
Lightning Source LLC
Chambersburg PA
CBHW050652270326
41927CB00012B/2992